CW00499964

Your Towns and Cities in the

Chatham in the Great War

'It was a gruesome task. Everywhere we found bodies in a terribly mutilated condition. Some had arms and legs missing and some headless. The gathering up of dismembered limbs turned one sick. It was a terrible affair and the old sailors, who had been in several battles, said they would rather be in ten Jutlands or Heliogolands than go through another raid such as this.'

(Ordinary Seaman Frederick W. Turpin, describing the aftermath of the German bombing raid at Chatham Barracks, 3 September 1917.)

Your Towns and Cities in the Great War

Chatham in the Great War

Stephen Wynn

Pen & Sword
MILITARY

First published in Great Britain in 2017 by
PEN & SWORD MILITARY
an imprint of
Pen and Sword Books Ltd
47 Church Street
Barnsley
South Yorkshire S70 2AS

ISBN 978 1 47382 788 2

A CIP record for this book is available from the British Library

Printed and bound in England
by CPI Group (UK) Ltd, Croydon, CR0 4YY

Typeset in Times New Roman by Chic Graphics

Pen & Sword Books Ltd incorporates the imprints of
Pen & Sword Archaeology, Atlas, Aviation, Battleground, Discovery, Family History, History, Maritime, Military, Naval, Politics, Railways, Select, Social History, Transport, True Crime, Claymore Press, Frontline Books, Leo Cooper, Praetorian Press, Remember When, Seaforth Publishing and Wharncliffe.

For a complete list of Pen and Sword titles please contact
Pen and Sword Books Limited
47 Church Street, Barnsley, South Yorkshire, S70 2AS, England
E-mail: enquiries@pen-and-sword.co.uk
Website: www.pen-and-sword.co.uk

Contents

	Sources	6
	Prologue	7
1	1914 – Starting Out	11
2	1915 – Deepening Conflict	27
3	1916 – The Realization	43
4	1917 – Seeing it Through	59
5	1918 – The Final Push	77
6	Some Who Returned	93
7	War Memorials	121
	Postscript	133
	Index	147

Sources

Commonwealth War Graves Commission
British Newspaper Archive
Wikipedia
Chatham Observer Newspaper
Violent Crime in England 1919 – Clive Emsley
Kitchener's Army – The raising of the New Armies 1914-1916 – Peter Simpkins
Women at War Gazette

www.1914-1918.invisionzone.com
www.regimentalrogue.com
www.ancestry.co.uk
www.naval-history.net
www.kenthistoryforum.co.uk
www.roll-of-honour.com/kent
www.thedockyard.com
www.kentww1.com/chatham
www.kentfallen.com
www.ancestry.co.uk
www.wrecksite.eu
www.kent.gov.uk
www.historylearningsite.co.uk

Prologue

Chatham is a long established town having first been officially recorded in 880 AD, when it was spelt slightly differently, as Cetham. It is one of the Kent towns which sit along the A2 road, which in Roman times was known as the Celtic route, although the Anglo-Saxons referred to it as Watling Street.

For centuries it remained no more than a village, but by the sixteenth century that changed when during the reign of Queen Elizabeth I, in 1568, a Royal Dockyard was built at Chatham. Originally it was only intended as a refitting base for ships of the British Royal Navy, but over time it developed into a major military shipbuilding yard. During its working lifetime, literally hundreds of vessels were built and launched from there.

Such was the dockyard's importance to the British establishment that a number of defensive fortifications were built around it to protect it from attack. King Henry VIII had ordered a fort to be built at what is now Sheerness, as a defensive structure at the mouth of the River Medway, to prevent the naval dockyards at Chatham from being attacked by enemy shipping. Any belief that such an attack wasn't possible, was dispelled by the Dutch raid which took place along the River Medway between 9 and 14 June 1667 during the Second Anglo-Dutch War, when a fleet of sixty Dutch ships and 1,500 Marines under the command of Lieutenant-Admiral Michiel de Ruyter, first attacked and then captured the Kent town of Sheerness, destroying the town's fort which was in the process of being strengthened, before sailing on to Chatham. Once there they set fire to and destroyed, thirteen Royal Navy vessels. Not satisfied with that, they 'stole' both HMS *Unity* and HMS *Royal Charles,* the flagship of the Royal Navy, and towed them back to Holland as prizes.

Not only was this a massive blow to the pride of the British as a nation, but it still rates as one of the worst defeats in the entire history of the Royal Navy. King Charles was somewhat embarrassed, as well as being a tad miffed by the Dutch actions in attacking the British along the River Medway, as at the time both sides had entered into peace negotiations in an attempt to end the conflict. One of the more staggering facts about the Dutch attack was that the British, through intelligence reports, had been aware that such an attack was likely to take place, but despite being in possession of this information, they did nothing to bolster their defences in and around the Kent area, with most of the British ships being at anchor off Harwich and further up the coast, in Scotland.

Throughout the seventeenth and eighteenth centuries there were political as well as military rumblings taking place throughout Europe on an almost continual basis making the threat of war or invasion, perceived or otherwise, never far from people's minds. This resulted in the fortifications in and around the Chatham area being both increased and improved, the work having begun in 1756. They were strategically placed rather than just randomly set down, but within fifty years even more forts were built for the defence of the area, and fifty years later, in the aftermath of the Royal Commission on the Defence of the United Kingdom, even more forts were constructed including Fort Luton, Fort Borstal and Fort Bridgewood.

Fortunately with Kitchener Barracks, the Royal Marine Barracks, Brompton Artillery Barracks and Melville Barracks, there were plenty of places to house the soldiers that were needed to man all of the forts. Chatham has a long and illustrious military history dating back hundreds of years, but it is mainly for its naval background that it is best remembered.

The Royal Navy Barracks at Chatham were known as HMS

Pemboke, the name taken from one of the naval ships moored at Chatham Dockyards. The other was HMS *Collingwood*.

The barracks had been built on land, which had previously been home to an old convict prison and a torpedo factory, at a cost of £500,000, and contained sufficient living quarters for between 3,000 and 5,000 officers and ratings. They were ready for occupation by January 1903. Prior to this time naval depot ships that were anchored at the naval dockyards at Chatham were used for accommodating those who were either undergoing their initial naval training or who were there on a course.

At the outbreak of the war in August 1914, 205 ships of the Royal Navy, along with their crews, were part of what formed the Chatham Division, which was stationed, not surprisingly, at Chatham.

North of Chatham at Lodge Hill on the outskirts of the village of Chattenden, was a pre-war anti-aircraft site. Its importance greatly increased with the outbreak of the First World War, being in an ideal location to provide cover to the Royal Navy base at nearby Chatham from potential aerial bombardment by either German aircraft or Zeppelins.

CHAPTER 1

1914
Starting Out

It was already being mooted in the early weeks of the war that it would all be over by Christmas, because once the British Tommy had given the Germans a good old fashioned bloody nose, they wouldn't want to know anymore. But sadly in those last five months of 1914, about 37,000 UK and Dominion servicemen and some civilians lost their lives, a strong indicator that Germany was not going to be the easy pushover that many people had initially suggested.

One of the main reasons for such heavy casualties was the tactics that were employed, especially by Germany and France, whose generals still appeared to favour large scale frontal assaults. These attacks were simply based on sending large numbers of their soldiers running head first, as fast as they could, towards enemy-held positions whose defensive strategy was based upon a number of strategically placed, murderous machine-gun positions that were spewing out thousands of rounds of ammunition towards their attackers. It turned no man's land into killing fields.

Back home in Chatham the sight of military personnel in uniform was nothing new for local residents, after all, there had been a naval dockyard in the town for 400 years. The Fort Pitt Military Hospital at Chatham had been treating wounded British soldiers from the early days of the war. Once their wounds had been treated they were moved on to nearby VAD Hospitals, where they could spend time convalescing, enabling them to make a full recovery. This in turn released urgently needed hospital beds for incoming wounded soldiers who had been sent back from the front.

The *Kent & Sussex Courier* dated Friday, 13 November 1914, carried the following article:

> *'HOLLINGBOURNE WORKHOUSE UTILISED FOR WOUNDED*
>
> *Some thirty-five wounded British wounded "Tommies" are now convalescent enough to leave Fort Pitt Military Hospital, Chatham, and have been sent to Maidstone and District. Nineteen, represented eighteen regiments from England, Scotland and Ireland, are at Hollingbourne Workhouse, which is probably the first Workhouse in England to accommodate British wounded. Sixteen are placed under the care of the VAD Hospital at Hayle Place. All the men are perfectly happy in their new surroundings. The majority came from the trenches at Armentieres, on the coast battle, and are shot in the hands and legs.'*

Fort Amherst

In 1715 the Duke of Marlborough ordered that a survey be carried out of the defensive needs of the Chatham area, which in essence saw the beginning of what became Fort Amherst. Over the years the original defences were added to and when the Napoleonic wars broke out in 1803 the government provided a large sum of money to enable the fortifications to be greatly improved. The building work would continue for another eight years, whilst the war would continue with the French, under the command of the Emperor Napoleon Bonaparte, until 1815.

Throughout the next hundred years the fort would see highs and lows, which would include improvements as well as a reduction in its military needs, with parts of the fort being demolished in 1878.

With the outbreak of the First World War Fort Amhurst was taken out of mothballs and used extensively as a holding post for soldiers and their equipment who were mustering in Kent in readiness for their deployment to France and Belgium.

Fort Pitt Military Hospital

Fort Pitt was built long before the start of the First World War, in fact by 1914 it had already been in existence for 102 years. Work had begun on it in 1805, and took seven years to complete. Its location was not just some random accident. Along with the other nearby forts, Amhurst and Clarence, it was built on high ground overlooking the River Medway, to form part of Chatham's defences against an invading aggressor. The town's dockyard was a particularly important military asset, one that needed defending at all costs, remembering of course that in 1805, Great Britain was still at war with Napoleon's France.

The first military occupants of the fort were the Royal Marine Artillery, who were in residence between 1814 and 1815. It was only because of the Battle of Waterloo that the fort began its long and industrious life as a military hospital, when it started looking after returning wounded British soldiers. From 1828 soldiers who had been badly injured in the service of the Crown were sent to Fort Pitt, which became a central unit for soldiers who had suffered such life-changing injuries. After building work on additional hospital accommodation had been completed in 1847, a lunatic asylum was added to the fort.

During the Crimean War it was once again used as a military hospital for wounded and sick soldiers returning from the fighting. Such was its military importance at the time, that the medical facility was visited by Queen Victoria and Prince Albert on more than one occasion, whilst the famous pioneer of professional nursing and medical statistics, Florence Nightingale, set up the first ever Army medical school there.

By the outbreak of the First World War, Fort Pitt had become an established military hospital, specifically set aside to deal with

Fort Pitt Military Cemetery Chatham.

wounded, sick and injured soldiers. It was open throughout the war in that capacity, finally closing for business in 1919, after the last of the wounded men had left and it was no longer economically viable to keep it open.

Today, some of those original buildings still survive and the site they stand on is now occupied by the Fort Pitt Grammar School.

Those servicemen who died of their wounds whilst being treated at Fort Pitt Military Hospital, were in the main buried at Fort Pitt Military Cemetery. There are 266 First World War graves in the cemetery, which was originally owned by the War Department.

The first burial in the cemetery from the Great War was that of Private (6737) Walter Henry Smith of the 6th Battalion, Duke of Cambridge's Own (Middlesex) Regiment, who died on 18 August 1914. He was born in Enfield and had enlisted at Mill Hill in Middlesex on 24 July 1913.

What made Walter's death even more poignant was how he was killed. He did not die on the battlefields of France or Belgium, he hadn't even left these shores; his death was a tragic accident. He was on guard duty in Chatham when another sentry accidentally dropped his rifle, which went off, the bullet striking Walter in his side; he died of his wounds soon afterwards. At the subsequent inquest, a verdict of accidental death was returned. The name of the soldier whose weapon it was or what action if any, was taken against him, are not recorded.

The last of the 266 servicemen to be buried in the cemetery was 29-year-old Bombardier W.J. Britton (1403133), of the Coastal Artillery School, Royal Garrison Artillery. He was a married man from the Cardiff area, who died on 16 July 1921.

The burials, which took place over a seven year period from 1914 to 1921, were spread out as follows:

1914: Fifteen
1915: Fifty-Seven
1916: Seventy
1917: Forty-Five
1918: Forty-Five
1919: Nineteen
1920: Eleven
1921: Four

As can be seen from the above figures, the four busiest years were 1915 until and including 1919, when a total of 179 burials of military personnel took place at the cemetery. The men buried there were serving with numerous regiments from all over Great Britain, Australia, New Zealand, and Canada.

Strangely enough the local pre-war newspapers for Chatham didn't cover the build up to the outbreak of war in any great detail, and although it wasn't exactly a total shock to residents of the town when the fighting began, there was a certain feeling of disbelief. It has to be remembered that before the war Chatham was, and had been for many years, a military and naval community that was more than used to seeing large numbers of men in uniform in their midst.

In the early months of the war leading up to Christmas 1914, Chatham was no different from the rest of the country. Patriotism was to the forefront of everyone's mind and men were willingly joining up to go off and 'do their bit for king and country'. Some young men who had never left the communities they had been born into, saw the war as an adventure, the chance to be part of something that people would be talking about for generations to come. Some saw it as their duty as men to go off and fight, whilst others saw it as the honourable thing to do.

They all wanted to be part of it, especially as the belief that 'it would all be over by Christmas' had been proffered by both politicians and the press. At the time nobody had the slightest idea that the war would go on as long as it did, or that so many young men would end up being killed before it was over.

During the five months between the outbreak of the war and 31 December 1914, a total of 37,607 British and Dominion men had been killed, an average of 7,521 men per month, or 246 men every single day. The total included 4,480 men of the Royal Navy as well as 33 men from the Royal Navy Volunteer Reserve; a number of these men would have been from Chatham or had some kind of connection with it.

Out of the total number of men who had been killed, 7,697 of them had been buried in cemeteries throughout the United Kingdom, which made the war very real indeed. These figures did not of course include the tens of thousands of men who had been wounded during the same period of time.

English wounded reach Chatham

On 6 August 1914 HMS *Amphion*, a light cruiser, hit a mine and sank, becoming the first ship of the Royal Navy to be sunk during the First World War. A total of 146 of her crew were killed whilst 160 survived and were rescued from the cold waters of the North Sea.

The previous day the *Amphion*, along with other vessels of the 3rd Flotilla, were engaged in a pre-arranged search for enemy shipping in a particular area of the North Sea, when they were informed by a British fishing trawler that they had earlier seen a suspicious vessel 'throwing things overboard'.

The *Amphion* made a note of the suspicious vessel's last known position and went off in search of it. Shortly afterwards they came across the SMS *Künigin Luise*, a German minelayer. Before the war she had been a passenger vessel running between Hamburg and the Netherlands, but the Germans had commandeered it and converted it in to a minesweeper. Despite the *Künigin Luise*'s attempt at disguise as a steamer of the Great Eastern Railway, she was caught and sunk by vessels of the 3rd Flotilla. Out of a crew of 100, only 46 German sailors survived, some of whom were picked up by the *Amphion*. At 0630 hours on 6 August 1914, whilst on her way back to her base at Harwich, the *Amphion* struck a mine which had been laid the previous day by the *Künigin Luise*. Eighteen of the German sailors who were rescued after she sank, perished when the *Amphion* went down.

The wounded sailors arrived at Chatham on 10 August 1914 in motor ambulances which had previously been used as London buses. Initially they became patients in the temporary military hospital in the aptly named Military Road.

Alleged Fraud

An article appeared in the *Daily Herald* dated 14 August 1914, concerning a fraud that had been carried out by Austin Mostyn Earle, whilst posing as a naval officer in full uniform. Having been charged with obtaining food by fraud at a Chatham hotel, and for obtaining the use of a motor vehicle under false pretences, he was committed for trial at Chatham.

The evidence against Earle was that when he arrived at the hotel he ordered a sumptuous meal, washed down with both wine and liqueurs and even had the temerity to order cigars to finish his lunch. Afterwards he carried on his charade by obtaining the use of a car by false pretences and actually paid a visit to the Royal Naval Barracks in the town, stating that he had an appointment with Mr McKenna, the Home Secretary's brother, and was saluted by the sentries on his arrival. How his fraud came to light isn't known.

Priest becomes Special Constable

Even the Church did its bit for the war effort on the home front. The Rev. H.R. Langton didn't just eulogise about the rights and wrongs of the war from his pulpit, he enrolled as a Special Constable at Chatham, and was attached to their motor cyclist section.

Hurled to death

The *Framlingham Weekly News* reported in its edition dated 22 August 1914 on the inquest relating to the death of two workers at the Chatham Naval Dockyard.

William Thomas Stowell, aged 47 and James McSweeney, who was 28, were both killed in the fitters department of the dockyard. The two men were employed as skilled labourers and were in the process of repairing a driving belt, when Stowell became entangled in the belt and was dragged round the revolving shafting at such a speed that he was hurled into the ceiling of the building with so much force that both his arms and legs were torn from his body.

In an effort to save his friend, McSweeney was knocked off of the platform that both men had been standing on, hitting his head on the ground as he fell, resulting in his death from a fractured skull.

McSweeney lived at 48 Henry Street, Chatham, with his parents, James and Rose McSweeney, and his seven brothers and sisters. One of his brothers, Ephraim, aged 19, enlisted in the Army on 2 September 1914 in London, literally only a matter of days after his brother James had been tragically killed. Initially he became a private (13449) in the 6th Battalion, Northamptonshire Regiment.

He served in France twice. Firstly between 25 July 1915 and 17 August 1916, and the second occasion was between 14 June 1917 and 22 November 1917. He had been wounded twice during his wartime service. On 1 July 1916, the first day of the Battle of the

Somme, he received gunshot wounds to his right thigh and arm which saw him admitted to the 22nd General Hospital in Dannes Camiers, in France, where he stayed for two days. On 19 November 1917 he received a shrapnel wound to his left hand, which in essence, ended his war, three days later he was sent home to England to have his wounds treated, where he would stay for the rest of the war.

After returning from his first tour of duty in France, he was a patient at the Mile End Military Hospital in London on 22 August 1916, when he was serving with B Company, 6th Battalion, Northamptonshire Regiment.

Whilst a patient at Horton War Hospital in Epsom in 1918, he was charged with being 'Absent without leave while on Active Service' for a period of two hours on the evening of 26 March 1918. Where he went or what caused him to be absent is not clear, but his punishment was the forfeiture of one day's pay. Despite this infringement, five days later he was granted a ten-day furlough from 31 March to 9 April 1918.

Ephraim survived the war and was demobbed on 6 April 1919 at Warley Barracks in Brentwood, Essex. At this time he was a private (57751) in the 17th (Depot) Battalion, Essex Regiment and his home address was then shown as being at 73 Chesterton Terrace, Plaistow, London.

He had another brother, Charles McSweeney, who also served in the Army during the war. He was a sergeant (775) in the 6th (Inniskilling) Dragoon Guards and was already serving in the Army at the time of the 1911 Census, when he was stationed in India. He first arrived in France on 16 December 1914. He was killed in action on 10 October 1918, and is buried at the Vis-en-Artois British Cemetery at Haucourt in the Pas-de-Calais region of France.

Winston Churchill visits Chatham

Winston Churchill, First Lord of the Admiralty, paid a morale-boosting visit to Chatham on Sunday, 30 August 1914, where he inspected the Royal Navy's cruiser, HMS *Arethusa* as well as the two destroyers HMS *Liberty* and HMS *Laurel*. All three vessels had been damaged during the Battle of Heligoland Bight which took place on 28 August.

He congratulated both the officers and men from all three ships, for a job well done and the determined and stoic manner in which they fought. He also made a point of shaking the hand of Private Irving, a member of the Royal Marine Artillery section, who was on board HMS *Arethusa* and who fired a total of 142 shots from a 7-inch gun during the course of the battle.

Two hundred German sailors, mainly from the cruiser *Mainz*, were picked up by ships from the Royal Navy and taken to Chatham. Those who were able bodied were interned, whilst those who were injured were sent to the Chatham Naval hospital for treatment.

Some of the local men wounded during the battle were: Leading Seaman Peter Whyte; Able Seaman George Robert Southby; Stoker, First Class Eugene O'Brien; Stoker, First Class Herbert William Henry Kemp; Stoker George William Calicutt Way; Stoker James M'Cardle and Stoker, First Class James Oriner. All of these men had served on board HMS *Laertes*.

Sinking of HMS *Aboukir*, HMS Cressy and HMS *Hogue*

Otto Eduard Weddigen was a Kapitanleutnant in the German Kaiserliche Marine and in command of the German submarine *U-9*, when on 22 September 1914, it sank three British warships of the 7th Cruiser Squadron in less than an hour, in the southern part of the North Sea. By the end of the action, besides the loss of the three ships, the British had also lost 62 officers and 1,397 men. Their loss caused a public outcry as well as damaging the Royal Navy's reputation. fortunately 837 men survived.

For his actions that day, Weddigen was awarded the Iron Cross, both second and first class. He commanded *U-9*, from 1 August 1914, until 11 January 1915.

The three British ships formed part of the Royal Navy's 7th Cruiser Squadron, a blockading force, whose main function was to stop German shipping from entering the English Channel. They were supported by destroyers of the Harwich Force in preventing the German Navy entering the Channel via the North Sea.

At the start of the war, many observers, some from the ranks of the Royal Navy, did not take the potential German submarine threat seriously enough.

The weather in the English Channel overnight on 21 September 1914 had not been good and certainly not conducive to sailing the high seas. By 0600 on the morning of 22 September, the rain and stormy seas had calmed, allowing the British ships to patrol at a steady 10 knots. Collectively they were following operational procedures. They had lookouts posted, searching for enemy ships or the telltale signs of submarine telescopes, and each of the three ships had guns on either side armed and manned.

In the meantime, and unbeknown to the British, the German submarine *U-9*, had been instructed to identify and attack any British transport ships it came across coming out of Ostend, but because of the storm on the night of 21 September, *U-9* had been forced to dive. By sheer luck when she surfaced she spotted the three British ships. Without wasting any time *U-9* opened fire on the nearest ship, which turned out to be HMS *Aboukir*. The time was 0620 hours. The torpedo struck the ship on the starboard side, flooding the engine room.

As no submarines or torpedoes had been spotted *Aboukir*'s Captain John Drummond assumed that his ship had struck a mine, and so requested that *Cressy* and *Hogue* come to his aid and help take off the crew from his sinking ship. Within thirty minutes of being hit the *Aboukir* had capsized and sunk.

U-9, still with the cover of the sea on her side, used her periscope to peruse the results of the damage caused by her first torpedo. Weddigen could see the ship he had hit with his first torpedo was in some distress and that two other British cruisers were in the process of trying to pick up survivors. As *Hogue* approached her sinking sister ship, her Captain, Wilmot Nicholson, realized that it had been a submarine attack and signalled the *Cressy* to look for a periscope, while his ship continued to close on *Aboukir* and her crew threw overboard anything that would float to aid the survivors in the water.

Having stopped and lowered all of her boats, *Hogue* was struck by two torpedoes around 0655. The sudden weight loss of the two torpedoes caused *U-9* to broach the surface and *Hogue*'s gunners opened fire without effect before the submarine could submerge again. The cruiser capsized about ten minutes after being torpedoed and sank at 0715.

Cressy attempted to ram the submarine, but did not succeed and resumed her rescue efforts until she too was torpedoed at 0720. Weddigen had fired two torpedoes from his stern tubes, but only one hit. *U-9* had to manoeuvre to bring her bow around with her last torpedo and fired it at a range of about 550 yards (500m) at 0730. The torpedo struck the port side and ruptured several boilers, scalding the men in the compartment. As her sister ships had done, *Cressy* took on a heavy list and then capsized before sinking at 0755. Several Dutch ships began rescuing survivors at 0830 and were joined by British fishing trawlers before Tyrwhitt and his ships arrived at 10.45. From all three ships 837 men were rescued but 62 officers and 1,397 enlisted men lost their lives; 560 of those lost were from *Cressy*.

Sinking of HMS *Bulwark*

HMS *Bulwark* was a pre-dreadnought style battleship which had been built at Devonport Dockyard, Plymouth for the Royal Navy. She was launched on 18 October 1899, began her sea trials in May 1901 and was commissioned on 11 March 1902.

Following the outbreak of the war, HMS *Bulwark* and the rest of the vessels that had previously formed the 5th Battle Squadron, as part of the Royal Navy's Home Fleet, found themselves attached to the Channel Fleet whose job it was to patrol and protect the English Channel.

On 26 November 1914, whilst at anchor in the River Medway off Sheerness, she suddenly exploded without any prior warning. Out of the crew of 750 officers and men, only sixteen members of

HMS Bulwark.

the crew initially survived, although seven of these later died in hospital.

Although the *Bulwark* was not sunk at Chatham, a number of the crew were from Chatham, which meant that many women and children from the town were subsequently without a husband and father. Forty-three of the crew who were killed in the explosion are buried at Gillingham (Woodlands) Cemetery.

Those who initially survived were:

Seaman C 3695, Royal Navy Reserve, James Anderson
Officers Steward 2nd Class L 5829, Frederick George Andrews
Able Seaman 238557, William Archibald Crow
Sergeant 8314, Albert Cosham Budd
Stoker 2nd Class K 21477, William Ewart Gladstone Day
Stoker 1st Class K 17693, Fred Goodlad Duffy

Stoker 1st Class 283372, Anthony Eames
Able Seaman 166068, James John Gale
Private 15744, Gilbert Lionel Guy
Leading Seaman 198355, William Johnson
Able Seaman 231657, Stephen Frederick Marshall
Able Seaman J 7172, Charles Pitter
Able Seaman 205028, Frederick Charles Spackman
Able Seaman 226097, James Strait
Leading Seaman 224279, Thomas William Strotten
Able Seaman 161786, Norman Stroud

Of those who initially survived, the following subsequently died of their wounds:

Thomas William Strotten died the same day in Chatham Hospital.
William Archibald Crow died the following day on 27 November.
Gilbert Lionel Guy died on 28 November.
Anthony Eames died on 29 November.
James Anderson and Frederick George Andrews, both died on 30 November.
James John Gale, survived for nearly seven weeks, until 18 January 1915.

Most of the remaining nine survivors received serious injuries.

It was 7.50am on 26 November 1914 when a huge internal explosion ripped apart the *Bulwark*, while she was anchored at No. 17 buoy in what is known as Kethole Reach, some four nautical miles west of Sheerness.

Members of the crews on board nearby ships, the battleships, *Prince of Wales* and *Agamemnon*, all reported that they first saw smoke coming from the stern of the *Bulwark*, and only after that did they see or hear any explosions, the first of which appeared to come from one of the rear magazines.

When Navy divers went down to take a look at the wreck on the seabed on 29 November, they saw that the explosion had been so powerful that a large section of the ship simply could not be identified. At the time of the explosion it was the most catastrophic accidental explosion in British maritime history, surpassed only by a similar explosion on board HMS *Vanguard*, three years later at Scapa Flow on 9 July 1917.

A naval court of enquiry that was convened two days after the ship was sunk, established that contrary to naval regulations, 275 6-inch shells had been placed close together, some so close that they were actually touching each other, in cross passageways which linked the ship's eleven magazines. The court of enquiry accepted that the most likely cause of the explosion was the overheating of cordite charges that had been stored alongside a boiler room bulkhead.

The wreck of the *Bulwark*, which is still on the seabed where it sunk, is now a designated and controlled site under the Protection of the Military Remains Act 1986.

CHAPTER 2

1915
Deepening Conflict

For the year 1915 British and Dominion forces lost a total of 151,765 men, who were either killed in action, died of their wounds or who fell victim to either illness or disease. There would have been at least twice as many more men who were wounded during the same period of time.

During the first five months of the war, in the second part of 1914, some thirty-eight major battles took place in places as far apart as China, East Prussia, the Falkland Islands and, of course, France and Belgium on the Western Front. Throughout 1915, there were only thirty-seven major battles, again in all theatres of war including Gallipoli, Italy, Poland and most notably in France and Flanders. This isn't of course a direct comparison as not all of the battles lasted for the same period of time, but it still makes for a shocking figure.

The first full year of the war saw Allied and Commonwealth forces incur some very heavy losses, these included the Battle of Loos, the Battle of Hill 60, the landings at Suvla Bay as well as those at Helles and Anzac Cove in Gallipoli, the Second Battle of Ypres, the Battle of Neuve-Chapelle, and the Battle of Dogger Bank.

The year could not have had a worse start with the loss of the Royal Navy battleship, HMS *Formidable*, on Friday, 1 January

Post card of HMS Formidable.

1915, when she was sunk whilst on exercises in the English Channel by two torpedoes fired by the German submarine, *U-24*.

HMS *Formidable* was part of the Royal Navy's 5th Battle Squadron which was based from 14 November 1914 at Sheerness, at the mouth of the River Medway, with its principal role being to prevent a possible German naval invasion of the United Kingdom.

On New Year's Eve 1914, the 5th Battle Squadron had taken part in a gunnery exercise off the Isle of Portland, south of Weymouth in Dorset. After the completion of the exercise the squadron's ships, including HMS *Formidable*, remained in the English Channel on patrol even though there had been reports of German submarines in the area. Weather conditions at the time were particularly hazardous, with heavy seas and high winds, which led to the belief that it would be extremely difficult for a submarine to carry out an effective attack in such inclement conditions.

The first of *U-24*'s torpedoes struck HMS *Formidable*'s number one boiler on the port side of the vessel, at approximately 0220 hours. Twenty minutes later Captain Noel Loxley gave the order to abandon ship, which was not easy to achieve in the darkness and with the ever-worsening weather conditions. At just after 0300 hours a second torpedo fired by *U-24*, once again struck the *Formidable*, this time on the vessel's starboard side.

Of the crew of 780 officers and men who were on board at the time of the attack, 35 officers, including Captain Loxley, and 512 men, were lost.

On the evening of 15 January 1915, at the Royal Naval Barracks Church, Chatham a memorial service was held in memory of those who were lost as a result of the sinking of HMS *Formidable*. The service was attended by Captain Loxley's widow and their young son, Peter. Some of the others present were the mayors of both Chatham and Gillingham, Colonel Lord Harris, Admiral Gaunt, as well as the Rev. A.T. Wallis, who was representing the Bishop of Rochester.

A number of those men lost in the tragedy, were from the Chatham and Gillingham areas.

Boy killed on the bed

On the night of 1 January 1915 the weather was particularly bad. A gale had wreaked havoc across the east coast of Kent, damaging homes and businesses as it went and ripping tiles and entire roofs from the properties which lay in its path.

Annie Smithson and her two children, Leslie aged 6, and daughter, Dorothy, aged 4, were lodgers with Mr and Mrs Hedgecock, at 17 Green Street, Gillingham. Annie's husband, Charles Henry Smithson, a sergeant (10248) in the 8th Signal Company, Royal Engineers, was away in France as part of the British Expeditionary Force.

Leslie and Dorothy were asleep in an upstairs bedroom when the chimney pot was blown off the roof of the house, causing it to crash through the roof into the bedroom where the children lay. Leslie was killed but Dorothy was only slightly injured.

Sergeant Smithson, who survived the war, was already in the

South African War Memorial Arch Royal Engineer Brompton Barracks, Chatham.

Army before the outbreak of hostilities, and was stationed at Brompton Barracks in Chatham. He had been in France since 5 November 1914.

Fleet Paymaster's Death

Duncan Stuart Ogilvie Grant, aged 45 and a single man, was an officer in the Royal Navy. He was also the Fleet Paymaster, stationed at Sheerness, on board HMS *Duncan*, a pre-dreadnought class battleship. He died in his cabin on 22 January 1915 from a single gunshot which had been fired from a revolver he was handling.

At the time of his death, presumably suicide, HMS *Duncan*, which had been part of the 6th Battle Squadron, was preparing for a major refit at Chatham, which lasted until July. When it was completed on 19 July 1915, *Duncan* was recommissioned and became part of the 9th Cruiser Squadron.

Even though Duncan's parents, Donald and Anna Grant lived in Gillingham and Duncan was born there, he was buried at the Ford Park Cemetery in Plymouth.

Wilfred Alfred Turley

Wilfred Arthur Turley was not a local Chatham boy, but from the village of Penshurst, which is a parish in the Sevenoaks district of Kent, where he had lived his entire life, but like a lot of young men during the First World War, Chatham was to play a big part in his life.

Before the war Wilfred had been a 'garden boy' and an 'under gardener' for a Penshurst resident, Dr Louis E. Wood.

On 24 January 1915, still only 20 years of age, Wilfred applied to enlist in the Royal Navy and was given orders to attend the Recruiting Office in Whitehall, London the following day. He rose early, had breakfast and left for London, where he spent most of the day waiting at the recruiting office until he was eventually seen around four o'clock .

Later that evening, after having completed all the necessary paperwork, Wilfred, who by now was Stoker 2nd Class K/24072 Turley, was sent with a group of other young recruits to Chatham by train. On arrival at the station they were met by members of the navy's training staff, and marched off to the barracks. One of their first experiences of military life was to be told to take a prolonged bath, not one with hot water to sooth their weary and tired bodies after what had been for all of them, a very long day, but an old fashioned one, in cold water. Afterwards Wilfred was sent to bed without any supper. A day or two later he wrote a letter home to his parents outlining his first few days of military life in the Navy, and what he thought about his temporary new home in Chatham. He also explained that he had the worst cold he had ever had. Sadly the cold did not improve, in fact it became a lot worse and turned into pneumonia, which resulted in his being admitted to the Naval Hospital at Chatham. Despite the medical staff's best attempts at dealing with Wilfred's condition, he passed away on 23 February 1917.

How he contracted pneumonia is not known, but surely the combination of sitting in a bath full of cold water for a prolonged period of time, having not eaten anything for some hours, after perspiring from marching in heavy clothes and kit, coupled with the heightened excitement of the day and the anticipation of a new life, most definitely wouldn't have helped.

He was buried in the churchyard of the parish church of St Mary's in Speldhurst.

On 22 November the same year, Wilfred's older brother, Ernest George Turley, was called up as a private (150626) in the Army Service Corps. He survived the war and was demobbed on 8 August 1919.

The Reverend moves on

Having toiled in the working class area of St John's parish in the Dockyard area of Chatham since 1909, the Rev. L.D. Hammond, left to take up the duties of senior curate at St James Church in Tunbridge Wells. His position at St John's had been his first after having completed his studies at the Lincoln Theological College. His keen and practical interest in sport, particularly football, made him a popular figure among the young men of Chatham. One of the numerous roles of which he took upon himself, was that of the Chairman of the Rochester and District Church of England football league.

The Reverend L.D. Hammond.

Walter Hayes Pickering Richards

Although he was born in Gloucestershire on 20 May 1881, Walter had for many years been based in barracks at Chatham. At the time of his death he was a captain in the Chatham Battalion of the Royal Naval Division, Royal Marine Light Infantry having been commissioned as a second lieutenant on 1 September 1899 and promoted to lieutenant on 1 July 1900.

He served in the Far East on the Royal Navy's China Station on board both HMS *Goliath* and HMS *Glory*, between 1901 and 1903.

On the day of his promotion to captain on 13 December 1909, he also became the adjutant of the Royal Marine Light Infantry, Chatham Division, where he remained until 1914. He was awarded the King George V Coronation Medal issued in 1911, for his service at the coronation. On 5 July 1911 in Macroom, Ireland he married Mary Florence Clayes and they had two sons, Edward Percy Richards, who died soon after his birth in 1912, and John Richards, who was born on 12 February 1914 at Chatham.

Walter was part of the British Expeditionary Force's Royal Naval Division, which was involved in the Siege of Antwerp between 2 September and 10 October 1914, although Royal Naval Division did not arrive until 3 October. Belgian, French and British forces tried their best to hold out against an overwhelming German artillery bombardment on the Belgium city of Antwerp.

Walter was part of the Mediterranean Expeditionary Force that arrived at Gallipoli on 6 February 1915 and three months later he was killed in action on 3 May 1915 during an attack on Razor Back, in the Monash Valley at Gallipoli. He had just reached a Turkish position when he died from a burst of machine-gun fire. Sadly, he has no known grave and his name is commemorated on the Helles Memorial which is located on the very tip of the Gallipoli Peninsula and is in the form of a 30-metre high obelisk.

For his actions on the day of his death, Captain Richards was mentioned in despatches on 16 June 1915 by the General Officer Commanding the Royal Naval Division: 'Captain Richards led a most gallant attack up a precipitous hill at Gaba Tepe and met his death by Machine Gun fire upon reaching the enemy's position.'

Here was a man who, although not born in the town, subsequently spent a lot of time living there, it was also where his son grew up. Chatham should rightly be proud of him.

Military funeral

Prior to the outbreak of war, Sapper Thomas Henry Saunders of the Kent Fortress Battalion, Royal Engineers had been a member of the Territorials for four years, serving with the Southborough Company of the Kent Fortress Battalion. Since that time he had been stationed at Chatham.

Whilst off duty and walking into town with some of his colleagues, he had the misfortune to trip over a kerbstone, landing on his back and injuring his spine. He was immediately taken to the Fort Pitt Military hospital for treatment. Whilst a patient there he contracted an unknown illness and passed away on 31 July 1915. He was buried with full military honours at Southborough Cemetery after a short service at the nearby St Margaret's Church. The ceremony was well attended by friends, family, and colleagues who formed a guard of honour. At the graveside eulogies and affectionate tributes were read out by some of his comrades.

Sapper Thomas Henry Saunders.

The death of Private C. Debley

The Queen's Own (Royal West Kent Regiment) was directly connected to Chatham with the 3rd Battalion being stationed at Fort Darland in the town.

Private (L/10550) Charles Dibley enlisted on 5 November 1914 at Maidstone. Having completed his initial training, he was sent out to France, arriving there on 6 March 1915. The following month he was wounded during the fighting at Hill 60, when he was struck by shrapnel on the left side of his face and forehead. He was sent back to England for further treatment and to recuperate. When he had recovered sufficiently from his wounds, he returned to full military duties, which in the first instance was at Chatham. He fell ill with pneumonia and was admitted to Fort Pitt Military Hospital, where he died on 24 July 1915. He was just 19 years of age.

His elder brother James also served during the war with the Royal Horse Artillery, having enlisted on 29 March 1916 at Woolwich. He survived.

Found at Chatham

On 18 September 1915 two German officers, Lieutenant Otto

Thelen, aged 25 and a pilot with the German Flying Corps, and Hans Keilback, aged 23 and a lieutenant in the German Imperial Navy, escaped from the German officers' prisoner of war camp at Donnington Hall in Leicestershire, which had been requisitioned at the start of the war.

They made good their escape on the evening of Friday, 17 September 1917, by digging a tunnel, which began from the cellar of the camp's library, and ran for some 60 yards to the other side of a perimeter fence. They had hidden the large amounts of soil they had dug, in an adjoining cellar so that it would not be seen by prison guards. Sightings of the two men were reported in the Loughborough and Melton areas, but they managed to evade being captured and made their way south. In Melton Mowbray they called in at the Crown Hotel, making a request for milk, but instead they were given some lemonade.

A reward of £100 for the recapture two men was offered by the Metropolitan Police at Scotland Yard, which in part led to numerous reports of their believed location. At first it was thought that they had made good their escape and managed to cross the English Channel, but this proved to be incorrect, and five days later the pair were captured in Chatham. For Thelan this wouldn't be his only escape attempt during his incarceration in England during the war.

The men had been noticed by local people on their arrival in Chatham, who thought them to be acting suspiciously. The Police were informed and the prisoners were arrested and taken into custody.

Arms versus legs

There was an article in the *Birmingham Mail* on 18 September 1915 which went a long way to showing the depth of character and resilience of the British soldier. Even in the toughest of times and the most difficult of circumstances, humour can go a long way in winning the battle against the darkness and negativity of adversity. An excellent example of this was shown by the military personnel who were patients at the Fort Pitt Military Hospital at Chatham. As part of their convalescence they enjoyed the odd game of bowls every now and then. Each game that was played went under the heading of 'Arms versus Legs'. One team was made up of Tommies who had lost a leg, whilst their opponents were soldiers who had lost an arm.

Kent's PoWs – A county conference

Wednesday, 22 September 1915 saw a conference take place at Chatham Town Hall on the subject of Kent's prisoners of war who were being held in camps throughout Germany. The meeting was convened by Lord Harris and those in attendance were the mayors of the county's major towns, along with representatives from the local tradesmen's association. The purpose of the meeting was to look at the collecting and sending of parcels of both food and clothing to the county's young men who were being held captive in Germany.

Clothes that could be sent were mainly items of underwear, such as pants, socks and vests; gloves and scarves were also permitted. Any outer clothing that had previously been sent had been confiscated by the German authorities concerned that it might be used in relation to escape attempts. Although there were no restrictions on which food items could be sent to the prisoners, a reminder was given at the conference not to include bread in any of the parcels, as on previous occasions, by the time the bread had arrived at its destination, it was usually mouldy. Separate arrangements were made to have regular food parcels, containing bread, sent from Switzerland which allowed for a much quicker delivery time, and reduced the chances of the bread already being spoilt on its arrival.

These parcels undoubtedly saved the lives of many Allied servicemen who were being held captive in camps throughout Germany, some of which saw the men held in dire conditions. Even though there was always the risk that the contents of the parcels might be stolen by the camp guards, the chance to help sustain the PoWs was well worth the risk. At the time food was also scarce for the German civilian population as well as their military personnel. The alternative option of not sending any parcels through fear that some might be stolen, was not seen as a serious proposition.

Lord Harris.

Lord George Harris, who had convened the meeting, was an important local figure. In the sporting arena his credentials didn't come any higher, having not only represented both Kent and England at cricket, but also captaining both teams. This portrait of him hangs on the walls of Marylebone Cricket Club in London.

Politically, he was the Vice Lieutenant of Kent and had been responsible for raising the 10th (Service) Battalion, Queen's Own (Royal West Kent Regiment) at Maidstone on 3 May 1915, at the request of the Army Council.

Postcards from the Buffs Prisoners of War

The Mayor of Chatham, (Alderman W. Paine, JP) had, according to the *Whitstable Times & Herne Bay Herald* dated 16 October 1915, received a number of postcards from local men who were being held as prisoners of war in Germany. One of them was from Private A.F. Cooper, 2nd Battalion, The Buffs (Royal East Kent Regiment), who was being held at a hospital in Giessen, which is north of Frankfurt in central Germany. The postcard was dated 5 September 1915 and he wrote:

> *'I beg to acknowledge the receipt of your parcel, received on 2nd September. Sincerely thanking you for the same. I am pleased to be able to inform you that I am recovering from the effects of my wound. I shall be very pleased to see the end of the war, so that I may have the pleasure of seeing you again.'*

Lance Corporal J. Murdoch, also from the 2nd Battalion, The Buffs, who was a prisoner at Göttingen, in Lower Saxony wrote:

Giessen Prisoner of War Camp, Germany. (www.worcestershireregiment.com)

> *'Thank you very much for sending me such a useful parcel, which I received safely and have found most acceptable. It is very kind of you and the inhabitants of Chatham, for the contents are such that are not possible for us to get here.'*

Letter of thanks

The *Whitstable Times & Herne Bay Herald*, dated 23 October 1915, contained a brief article about Admiral Sir Richard and Lady Poore, who had written to Chatham Town Council thanking them for their kind and thoughtful message of sympathy at the loss of their only son, Lieutenant Roger Poore, during fighting in Flanders. He was 29 years of age and served with A Battery, 48 Brigade, Royal Field Artillery, when he was killed in action, whilst acting as a forward observation officer at Ypres, on 19 September 1915. He is buried at Duhallow Advanced Dressing Station Cemetery, which is situated in the West-Vlaanderen region of Belgium. The cemetery was not begun until July 1917, which means that originally Roger Poore, would have been buried elsewhere and his remains subsequently moved to their final resting place after the Armistice. It was quite common for soldiers to be buried on a battlefield close to where they had fallen.

Admiral Sir Richard Poore said in the letter to Chatham Town Council, *'It is a token of friendliness which sinks deep. At the same time we are proud to have given all we had for our country.'*

Between 1911 and 1915, he was the commander-in-chief of The Nore, a sandbank situated at the mouth of the River Medway. During those years, in line with his position, his residence was Admiralty House which was next to the naval barracks, HMS *Pembroke*, at Chatham.

Comforts for the West Kents

The edition of the *Kent and Sussex Courier* for 3 December 1915, included a letter of appeal from Lady Boscawen:

'Dear Sir,
Last winter you kindly inserted an appeal from me for comforts for the men of the 3rd Battalion, Royal West Kent Regiment, who were employed on guard duty at Chatham. This appeal was the means of providing a large number of comforts for those sentries who have to be on duty day and night. May I venture to make another appeal this year? Scarves to put round the neck and warm gloves and mittens for the hands are what are chiefly required.

Will those who are good enough to send parcels, direct them to The Quarter Master, 3rd Battalion, Royal West Kent Regiment, Fort Darland, Chatham.

Yours faithfully,
Edith G. Boscawen
80 Cornwall Gardens
London, SW.
Nov. 28th 1915.'

Lady Boscawen's husband, Colonel Sir Arthur Boscawen MP was the commanding officer of the 3rd Battalion, Royal West Kent Regiment. During December 1915 he had been in France and had visited a base camp at Rouen, before going up to the front and spending time attached to a battalion in the trenches. On his return to England he resumed his duties at Chatham.

Successfully recruiting at 78 years of age

In difficult and demanding times such as a war, some people simply fall by the wayside under the immense pressure which is placed upon them, whilst others just take it all in their stride and thrive on the burden of responsibility placed upon their shoulders. In December 1915 it was noted that one such person was most definitely doing his bit for the war effort, as well as his king and country. That man was William George who lived at The Retreat, 9 George Street in Chatham.

William was 78 years old and part of the Chatham Army recruiting team, under the guidelines as laid down by the Lord Derby scheme. This had been brought in during the autumn of 1915, in an effort to persuade eligible men who were between 18 and 41 years of age to enlist, with a promise that they would then not be called up until a later date, when their service was required.

Between November and December 1915 the scheme obtained a total of over 315,000 men who had committed themselves to enlisting, although there were also a large percentage of both single and married men who had refused to sign up. It was no coincidence therefore that the following year the Government introduced compulsory conscription for the first time, to ensure that they had sufficient large numbers of men available to fight.

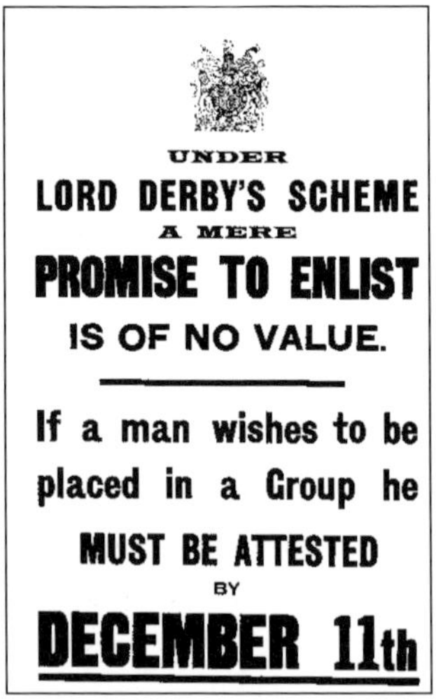

Lord Derby's Scheme.

William was a member of the National Reserve as well as a Special Constable in Chatham. He was a retired soldier who had served for twenty-one years with the Royal Field Artillery, finishing his military career as a sergeant. He had been in receipt of an Army pension for a staggering thirty-eight years, having retired in 1877.

The 1911 Census showed that William had two lodgers living at his home, both of whom were sailors stationed at Chatham. Thomas

Kelly who hailed from Hartlepool, was an Able Seaman in the Royal Navy, and Leading Seaman Alfred James Heath (205750), who was a Londoner and was also stationed at Chatham. Alfred had joined the Royal Navy as a boy and in 1901 he was serving on board HMS *Rattler* in Sierra Leone. He was then a 'Boy 1st Class'. Sadly Alfred was one of the crew who was killed when HMS *Aboukir* was sunk on 22 September 1914. He left a widow, Nellie Heath, who at the time was living at 121 Claude Road in Leyton.

One of William's three sons, William Henry George, was also a military man and, like his father, he had his own remarkable story. He had enlisted in the Royal Scots Fusiliers as a 14-year-old boy on 12 November 1897, when he signed up for twelve years with the colours. His previous occupation was shown as that of musician and he was just 4ft 7½ in tall. When he had served his time in 1909, rather than leave the Army he re-signed to stay and complete twenty-one years' service. When war broke out he was with the 1st Battalion which was stationed at Gosport. They were quickly mobilized and arrived in Le Havre on 14 August 1914 as part of the British Expeditionary Force. On 14 September he was reported missing during the fighting at the Battle of the Aisne, but the next day it was confirmed that he had been taken prisoner by the Germans. He would spend the rest of the war as a prisoner of war in Germany, finally being released from captivity on 17 December 1918 arriving back in England the next day. He was demobbed on 30 March 1919, having served for 21 years and 139 days, although four years and ninety-four days of that was as a prisoner of war.

There can't be too many examples of a father and son having both served in the British Army for 21 years – quite an achievement by anybody's standards.

An Archdeacon's Adventures

At the request of the Bishop of Rochester, Archdeacon Oswald William Charles Blogg (possibly spelt Blogue or even de Blogue) returned from Brazil to take up the wardenship of Navy House at

Chatham, arriving back in the country at Liverpool on 16 December 1916.

A few years earlier Archdeacon Blogg was a chaplain in the Royal Navy. One night, in order to understand the men's temptations ashore, he disguised himself as an ordinary seaman, visited pubs and in particular hung about The Brook pub near Military Road in Chatham, which unfortunately for the Archdeacon was out of bounds to all military personnel. He was subsequently seen and arrested by a Naval picket, which was similar to a military policeman.

This was obviously embarrassing for the Archdeacon as he now found himself in the somewhat awkward position of having to convince the naval authorities as well as the Bishop of Rochester that he hadn't suddenly lost his religious calling, but was simply carrying out some of his own research, so that he had a better understanding of the basic earthly needs of the men for whom he was tasked with providing religious direction. He was obviously an extremely good orator as his explanation would appear to have been accepted, albeit with the slight raising of one or two disbelieving eyebrows.

The Archdeacon was married, having taken Ethel Langley Hancock as his wife in April 1903 in Hampshire. They had a daughter, Eirene Nevill de Blogue, who was born on 10 August 1904 in Hythe.

It's not entirely clear when Oswald became a naval chaplain, but it was possibly on 1 December 1907, and at the time of the 1911 Census he is shown as being one of the crew of an un-named Royal Navy vessel, somewhere in the Mediterranean. As late as 6 January 1916 he is still recorded as an acting chaplain on temporary service.

Oswald died on 15 April 1959 aged 85 at East Court Nursing Home, Havant Street, Cosham, Hampshire. In his will, he left the sum of £9,079 10s 10d, a large sum of money. His wife Ethel, died in December 1965 in Gosport, Hampshire, aged 89.

CHAPTER 3

1916
The Realization

The war was now into its third year and still there was no sign of an end to the bloody slaughter with which it had become synonymous. Instead of the likelihood of an end to the fighting, 1916 would see an escalation, with death on both sides continuing on what was becoming an almost industrial scale.

There would be twenty-six major battles in 1916 including the Battle of the Somme which began on 1 July and carried on for over four months, until 18 November.

What was really shocking was the anticipated heavy losses that governments were not only expecting, but appeared willing and prepared to sustain. So appalling were some of the tactics employed by senior military officers, that heavy losses were almost inevitable. Largely because of this apparent 'couldn't care less', almost cavalier attitude towards the men who made up the vast majority of the rank and file soldiers, whom the British Government so greatly depended upon, the same life-sapping tactics continued. To deal with the need for more and more men to go and fight, rather than try and bring the war to an end by political means, compulsory military service was introduced in the shape of the Military Service Act 1916, ensuring the extra men needed would be readily available. It has to be remembered that the vast majority of those young men were being sent off to fight by a government which had not yet provided them with the right to vote. On the one hand they were expected to fight for their king and country, which could result in maiming or death, yet those under 21 and many poor men were disenfranchised.

Chatham Fire

On 15 January 1916 a large fire broke out at the Royal Engineers Barracks at Chatham. It was subsequently established that the seat of the fire was in the stable block which was underneath the men's accommodation block within the barracks. Miraculously, even though the fire was not discovered until many of the buildings had caught fire and were destroyed, not one of the horses was injured or lost, every one of them being removed to safety.

The fire brigades from Chatham and the nearby towns of Rochester and Gillingham all attended the barracks to assist the military, naval and dockyard brigades in extinguishing the fire, but not before it had caused thousands of pounds worth of damage. Thankfully there were no casualties.

Masters Lodge of Freemasons

Even in a time of war the civilian world carried on as usual, or as usual as it possibly could in the circumstances. One such organisation that continued with business as usual was the Masters Lodge of Freemasons, specifically Lodge No. 3173, which covered the Chatham area of Kent. Their meeting of 22 January 1916 was for the first time ever held outside Chatham, when it went ahead in Maidstone, but only after special dispensation to do so was granted by the Grand Lodge.

In charge of the meeting was Sir John Cockburn, whose Masonic title was that of the Right Worshipful Brother. Sir John was a doctor by profession and had also been a politician who on 27 June 1889, became the eighteenth premier of South Australia, even though by birth he was actually a Scotsman, born in Crosbie at Berwickshire in 1850.

Sir John Cockburn.

He had been initiated into the world of Freemasonry in 1876, and had helped establish the Grand Lodge of South Australia. There were upwards of one hundred members of the lodge in attendance at the meeting, who listened keenly to the lecture which Sir John gave, the topic of which was 'The Swastika', in which he discussed its possible connection with Freemasonry.

It would be another four years before the Nationalsozialistische Deutsche Arbeiterpartei – NSDAP – Nazi Party, was formed in Munich and the swastika would become their chosen symbol of identification.

HMS *Arethusa*

The *Arethusa* was built at Chatham Dockyard and launched on 25 October 1913. She was a light cruiser with a top speed of 28.5 knots

HMS Arethusa *being towed after striking a mine off Felixstowe.*

and her armaments included one anti-aircraft gun, two 152mm guns, six 102mm guns as well as four torpedoes.

After being commissioned in August 1914 she became part of the Harwich Force, whose job it was to prevent ships from the German Imperial Navy attacking vessels of the Royal Navy as well as those of the merchant fleet.

Although the *Arethusa* had a comparatively brief existence, she certainly had a busy one. On 28 August 1914 she took part in the first naval action of the war, the Battle of Heligoland Bight, which took place off the north-east coast of Germany, when British ships attacked a German patrol. The battle was a resounding victory for the British, but the *Arethusa* was badly damaged by two of the German cruisers and had to be towed back to her base. A total of fifty-five British sailors were wounded in the ensuing fighting with another thirty-five killed. As for the Germans, six of their ships were sunk with a further six being damaged in some way or another. They lost a total of 712 of their men, with another 149 who were wounded and a further 336 who were captured and taken prisoner.

After being repaired, the *Arethusa* was back to work and took part in the Cuxhaven Raid on Christmas Day 1914, when the Royal Navy took pre-emptive action by attacking German Zeppelins whilst they were moored at their base at Cuxhaven, so preventing them from carrying out attacks over Britain.

On 25 January 1915 she also took part in the Battle of Dogger Bank. Just over a year later on 11 February 1916 she struck a mine off Felixstowe. Whilst being towed back to her base at Harwich she drifted on to a sand bank and broke in half.

On the evening of 12 February 1916, some 300 surviving members of the *Arethusa* arrived at Chatham and were taken to the Royal Naval Barracks. They were all provided with new uniforms and equipment, and after a good night's sleep, they were home on leave.

The following list includes the men who were killed when the *Arethusa* struck a mine off Felixstowe, and whose names are recorded on the Chatham Naval Memorial:

Arthur **Allen**, Stoker 1st Class. S. No. K/23352.
Henry Richard **Andrews**, Stoker 1st Class. S. No. K/12672.
Charles Battlemore **Butcher**, Stoker 2nd Class. S. No. SS/117133.
James **Cummings**, Chief Stoker. S. No. 277894.
William **Harling**, Stoker. S. No.6934S.
Ernest Walter **Nicholls**, Stoker 1st Class. S. No. K/20737.
Richard **Robinson**, Stoker 1st Class. S. No. SS/108881.
Leonard **Sleeth**, Petty Officer Stoker. S. No. K/85.
James Thomas Andrew **Taylor**, Engine Room Artificer 2nd Class. S. No. 22070.
Ethelbert Palmer **Turner**, Petty Officer Stoker. S. No. 290487.
William George **Warne**, Mechanic. S. No. 293842.
Henry **Wightman**, Stoker 1st Class. K/21030.

All of these men are believed to have been in the ship's stokehole when the *Arethusa* struck the mine, and were killed outright. The mine had been laid by the German submarine *U-C7* only the previous evening.

The following is taken from *The Admiralty Regrets – British Warship Losses of 20th Century* by Paul Kemp.

'Mined in approach to Harwich off the North Cutle Buoy. Casualties 8 plus cat, survivors 272.

It was whilst returning from the abortive sweep for the German High Seas Fleet that the famous light cruiser was lost. She was steaming at 20 knots and had just entered the Sledway Channel when she struck a mine which had been laid by *UC7* the previous evening.

Six men were killed in the explosion and another two drowned when their Carley float overturned. Tyrwhitt was the last to leave the ship, having remained to look for his cat. After Tyrwhitt's boat had pushed off a bearded figure was seen to rush on to the quarterdeck. This was a stoker who had not only slept through the explosion but slept on through the subsequent activity. Trapped below he had clambered up the inside of the after funnel and then out on to the quarterdeck.'

Of the twelve men who were killed, 42-year-old Chief Stoker James Cummings was from Chatham, although he was originally born in Glasgow in 1874. He lived at 45 Albany Road in the Luton area of the town with his wife of seventeen years, Isabella, although she sometimes used the shortened name of Ella. They had four children: two sons, George and Hector, as well as two daughters, Ella and Ina.

A group of Kent men in the RAMC, including those from Chatham.

This photograph was taken on 27 March 1916 in France and is of a group of soldiers from the 103rd Field Ambulance Royal Army Medical Corps soldiers; all are from the Kent area, including Chatham.

From top to bottom and left to right, their names are:

Top Row:
(1) Private F. Hurrell
(2) Private Cecil James Bending
(3) Private H. Beney

Second Row:
(4) Private P. Piper
(5) Private Saunders
(6) Private H. Whiteland
(7) Private Wood
(8) Private Sydney John Bending
(9) Private Highfield

Third Row:
(10) Private Mee
(11) Lance Corporal Page
(12) Sergeant Brooker
(13) Sergeant Pocklington
(14) Lance Corporal Mack
(15) Private Green

Front Row:
(16) Private Hawkins
(17) Private Wilson
(18) Private T. Cavie
(19) Private Geo ?
(20) Private Stokes

Having arrived in France in January 1916, 'The Ambulance' quickly saw its fair share of active service, as they were often required to go up to the front line trenches to convey wounded soldiers to the field dressing stations which were situated immediately to the rear of the trenches. This work was mainly carried out under the cover of darkness, which provided the men with an element of safety, but caution still had to be applied as the roads which led up to the trenches were intermittently swept by German machine-gun fire.

On one occasion two of the men who were brothers, Private Sydney John Bending and Private Cecil James Bending, were temporarily stationed at a first aid post that was attached to an artillery unit. By the time they had finished there, the continuous noise and concussion of the huge British guns, was a memory that would stay with both of them for a very long time. A third brother, Claude W. Bending also served during the war with the 10th Battalion, Duke of Cornwall's Light Infantry. All three of them survived the war.

The Ambulance was for the most part situated in the La Crosse area, east of St Omer. There they also found themselves responsible for two field hospitals, which were very close to the front line trenches, each of which catered for between 150 to 200 wounded and sick men at any one time. To add to their woes they were visited on a regular basis by German aircraft, leaving the British unsure as to whether they were conducting reconnaissance flights or were on bombing raids. They didn't wait too long to find out which it was, however, deploying their own anti-aircraft guns in an offensive manner.

Major Francis John William Harvey VC.

Major Francis John William Harvey VC. Royal Marine Light Infantry

Major Francis John William Harvey was born on 29 April 1873 at Sydenham in south London, the only son of Commander John William Francis Harvey, Royal Navy and Elizabeth Edwards Lavington Harvey.

When he was 11 years old he moved with his parents to Southsea where he was enrolled at Portsmouth Grammar School. After finishing his secondary education he decided on a life in the military, specifically the Royal Navy, and was offered places at both the Royal Military College, Sandhurst and the Royal Naval College at Greenwich, for officer training. He decided on the latter school and trained to become a Royal Marine officer cadet, passing out in 1892 and becoming a lieutenant the following year, when he joined the crew of HMS *Wildfire*, for his first seagoing commission.

He came from a long line of military men, going back over four generations to his great-great-grandfather, John Harvey, who was killed in the naval battle against the French known as the Glorious First of June in 1794.

Major Harvey was posthumously awarded the Victoria Cross for his actions on 31 May 1916, whilst serving as an officer of the Royal Marine Light Infantry, on board HMS *Lion* during the Battle of Jutland. He had already seen action during the battles of Heligoland Bight and Dogger Bank. The *Lion* was struck by a shell fired by the German vessel, SMS *Lützow*, which hit one of the ship's gun ports, blowing its roof wide open and started a fire, killing or wounding all of the crew who had been stationed in the gun house. Harvey, although suffering from both wounds and burns, realised the potential catastrophic damage that the fire could cause to the *Lion*'s Q Turret, where tons of cordite was stored.

He gave orders for the magazine doors to be locked closed and then for the magazine department to be flooded to prevent the cordite and ammunition from being consumed by the fire and exploding. Harvey died of his wounds a short while later, but his actions undoubtedly saved the ship and the lives of a great many of the crew.

The citation for the award of Harvey's Victoria Cross which appeared in the *London Gazette* on 15 September 1916, read as follows:

'Major Francis John William Harvey, RMLI, whilst mortally wounded and almost the only survivor after the explosion of an

enemy shell in "Q" gunhouse, with great presence of mind and devotion to duty ordered the magazine to be flooded, thereby saving the ship. He died shortly afterwards.'

His name is commemorated on the Chatham Naval Memorial.

Spotted Fever among Military at Chatham

At the end of March 1916 there was an outbreak of spotted fever among military personnel in Chatham and the surrounding areas, which caused anxiety for the military authorities. The fever is a tick-borne disease, the effects of which come out on the skin, and are caused by bacteria of the *genus rickettsia*. It was first discovered in Tunisia in 1910 when it was given the name *boutonneuse* which is the French word for 'spotty'. The symptoms included headaches, chills, high fevers, muscular pain and a sensitivity to light.

The situation came about mainly because of the men's living conditions. A decision had been taken by senior officers that men from the 'other ranks', should be removed from their barracks and billets and live in the open under canvas tents throughout the early months of 1916, during what had been a particularly harsh winter. It was mainly as a result of this enforced direction that the spotted fever flourished so readily.

Senior officers, although expected to show leadership and compassion for their men, whilst at the same time setting an example, did not have to endure the same hardships.

Chatham Wood Tragedy

Both national and local newspapers were carrying reports in their pages at the end of October 1916, about the tragic murder of a 20-year-old woman by the name of Emily Maria Trigg.

As a child Emily lived with her parents, Kate and John Trigg, her two sisters, Elizabeth and Edith, as well as her five brothers, John, William, Harry, Frederick and Arthur, at Providence Row, Blue Bell Hill, Burham in Rochester.

Emily's father, John, a quarryman, had died at the relatively young age of 53 in 1915, leaving his widow, Kate, to bring up their two children, Arthur and Edith, who were still living at home.

On 6 August 1916, Emily, who by now was in service as a maid for Miss Catherine Cooper, was at her home at 36 Maidstone Road, Rochester.

36 Maidstone Road, Rochester, Kent.

Having finished her work at Miss Cooper's home about 3.15pm, she left to go and visit her mother who lived only a short distance away. It was a warm summer's afternoon and it would have made for a pleasant Sunday afternoon stroll. Sadly Emily never arrived at her mother's home and it would be another two days before it was realised that she was missing and the Police were informed. What enquiries they made and how much effort went in to trying to discover what had happened to her and where she might be, isn't clear.

Six weeks later on 21 September, John Jennings, a local greengrocer, was in Bridge Wood, which was next to Maidstone Road, picking blackberries with his two children, when he came across a human skeleton. It was that of Emily Trigg. Amazingly, the local Police had never searched the woods during their investigation into Emily's disappearance.

Newspaper articles of the time mentioned that a gold necklace, which had been identified as belonging to Emily, was found near to her body. Her clothes which had been both cut and stripped away, were found a short distance away, and some cut grass had been placed over the body. One newspaper included the following paragraph: *'Medical evidence tended to show there had been an attempt at outrage, but it was impossible to state the cause of death. Probably more than one person was concerned in the crime.'*

The phrase, *attempt at outrage*, strongly suggests that she had either been raped or that an attempt had been made.

On Stephen Rayner's website, entitled Medway Memories, mention is made of how quickly Emily's body decomposed. There are many factors which will determine this, including what the weather was like at the time. As it was relatively warm when Emily met her death, the bacteria in the body would have been able to survive a lot longer than if it had happened during the winter months. Compared with how long it would take a body to decompose that had been left out in the open today, six weeks does not seem long at all, but it has to be remembered that in Emily's case, we are talking of a hundred years ago, so a direct comparison is not entirely possible. One of the factors to consider is that because of the amount of processed food people now have as part of their everyday diet, which contain lots of preservatives, these over time build up in the body's system and actually slow down the process of decomposition when people die.

The inquest into Emily's death was opened within a matter of days of the discovery of her body, but was adjourned until 9 October 1916 at Chatham Town Hall, so as to provide the Police with enough time to carry out their enquiries. There it was stated that it was not possible to ascertain Emily's cause of death, mainly because the Police surgeon, Doctor Bryan, was unable to establish how she had died, but it was still treated as a murder and it has always been assumed that she was killed on 6 August 1916. Doctor Bryan also intimated that everything pointed to more than one person being concerned in Emily's death, but did not elaborate further on this point.

Emily carried a photograph of her boyfriend, George Harris, a private in the Royal West Surrey Regiment but he was eliminated as a suspect in the investigation very early on as he was in Shoreham hospital on 6 August. At the subsequent inquest, the jury, without confirmation that Emily had in fact been murdered, returned an open verdict.

Eleven days later on 20 October, Charles Hicks, a gunner in the Royal Garrison Artillery at Winchester, was arrested and charged on suspicion of being concerned in Emily's murder. He was subsequently held in custody until the following Tuesday, allowing the Police time to make their enquiries. Police Superintendent Rhodes informed the court that there would be no evidence offered against Gunner Hicks, who was released from custody with his reputation still intact.

On the Medway Memories website there is reference to Emily having told Miss Cooper that she was going out with a soldier, but because he was a gentleman and she was a country girl, she didn't like to be seen out with him. This would strongly suggest that if she was seeing a soldier other than her boyfriend, George Harris, this other man would have been an officer and not from the other ranks. Whoever killed Emily took her by surprise it was definitely not somebody who she had pre-arranged to meet, because she left Miss Cooper's house in time to get to her mother's home by 3.15. As no altercation was heard or witnessed by anyone, whoever Emily's assailant was must have quickly covered her mouth to stop her from screaming, and then dragged her backwards some 30 yards into the woods, before killing her.

The website also mentions that no bloodstains were found on Emily's clothes; this information coupled with the knowledge that the Police surgeon who had inspected Emily's body records nothing about having discovered any wounds, strongly suggests that she was either suffocated or strangled. He did, however, discover a piece of material from her clothing which had been stuffed in her mouth.

Emily Trigg's death remains a mystery. Although no evidence was ever produced that conclusively confirmed the cause of her death, the likelihood is that she was murdered rather than having died as the result of an accident. This being the case, her killer(s) have never been identified, nor the reason for her murder or how it was carried out. The other question is, was/were her killer(s) lying in wait to pounce on any unsuspecting female who just happened to wander by, or was/were he/they there because he/they knew the time and route that she would be walking.

Three of Emily's brothers are known to have served during the First World War, William, Frederick and John, although I was unable to establish which regiments they served with. The British Army's Medal Roll Index Cards, for the period of the First World War, shows thirty-two men who served in the Army with the name of William Trigg, four of whom served with the Royal Engineers and five who served with the Army Service Corps. There were eleven men with the name Frederick Trigg, two of whom served with the Devonshire Regiment and another two who served with the Queen's Own (Royal West Kent Regiment). There were also eleven men who served with the name of John Trigg.

Almost unbelievably, there were ten men with the name George

Harris, who served in the Queen's (Royal West Surrey) Regiment.

In relation to Charles Hicks, there is only one man with his name showing in the same records as having served with the Royal Garrison Artillery. His service number was 191648. What happened to either George Harris or Charles Hicks is not known.

The Chatham Elephant

The *Dover Express* newspaper dated 25 August 1916 included an article that they had taken from a 1915 Natural History Museum report. It was a good example of the other side of life and highlighted the point that although there was a war going on, the parallel world of everyday life was still running side by side:

> *'In the autumn of 1913 information was received from Mr Sydney Turner of Luton, Chatham, of a discovery of fossil bones in the grounds of the Royal School of Military Engineering at Upnor. Dr C.W. Andrews, an assistant in the Department of Geology, was sent to make an investigation on the spot, and was at once able to identify the remains as those of an elephant. The War Office and the Commandant gave permission to excavate the skeleton and remove it to the museum.*
>
> *During the dry season of 1914, the outbreak of war prevented the work, but in 1915 the excavation was proceeded with, and the specimen was successfully removed to South Kensington. The find proved to comprise the greater part of a skelton of Elephas Antique, which was one of the largest elephants that had ever been discovered in Britain, though of the skull only the molar teeth, one tusk, and part of the lower jaw are capable of preservation. The discovery is especially important as being the first occasion on which the skeleton of this species has been found in England in direct association of the teeth.'*

Sydney Turner, a skilled labourer, who originally discovered the remains of the elephant, lived at 10 Nelson Terrace, Luton, Chatham, with his wife Eliza and their two children.

CHAPTER 4

1917
Seeing it Through

The war that was originally going to be all over by Christmas 1914, had now entered its fourth year and still there was no sign of it ending. Most observers just wanted it over with, but that was easier said than done. Things had gone too far to just walk away, but its continuation required more and more men to enter the fray and the longer it went on, more and more lives would be lost.

Throughout 1917 a staggering total of 294,497 British and Dominion soldiers were either killed in action, or died of their wounds, illness or disease, and it is estimated that double that amount were wounded. That means on average 807 men died, every single day of the year; compare this to Britain's thirteen-year involvement in Iraq and Afghanistan, where 456 men and women lost their lives.

Twenty-nine major battles took place throughout 1917 on all fronts, and seven along the Western Front throughout France and Belgium as Allied and German forces flexed their muscles against each other. The Battle of Arras and the British offensive in Flanders, including the infamous Battle of Passchendaele, saw a continuation of fighting all the way through until mid-November and the Battle of Cambrai, which is noted for the first large scale use of tanks in modern warfare. In a seventeen-day battle, both sides incurred approximately 45,000 casualties, which averages out at 2,647 per day. The British also lost a total of 179 of their tanks.

Thomas Crisp VC

Thomas Crisp was awarded the Victoria Cross as well as the Distinguished Service Cross, and although not a Chatham man by birth, his name is included on the Chatham Naval Memorial as one of those who had lost their lives at sea during the First World War.

The *London Gazette* dated 2 November 1917, No. 30363, included the following report of Thomas Crisp's action which posthumously won him the award of the Victoria Cross.

Thomas Crisp wearing his Distinguished Service Cross.

'Action of H.M. Armed Smack "Nelson" on the 15th August, 1917.

On the 15th August, 1917, the Smack "Nelson" was engaged in fishing when she was attacked with gunfire from an enemy submarine. The gear was let go and the submarine's fire was returned. The submarine's fourth shot went through the port bow just below the water line and the seventh shell struck the skipper, partially disembowelling him, and passed through the deck and out through the side of the ship. In spite of the terrible nature of his wound Skipper Crisp retained consciousness, and his first thought was to send off a message that he was being attacked and giving his position. He continued to command his ship until the ammunition was almost exhausted and the smack was sinking. He refused to be moved into the small boat when the rest of the crew were obliged to abandon the vessel as she sank, his last request being that he might be thrown overboard.'

Thomas Crisp was born at Lowestoft in Suffolk on 28 April 1876, and was one of ten children to William and Mary Anne Crisp. He left a widow, Harriet, and their three young children, Harriet and Thomas and William.

Thomas had been a fisherman most of his adult life and at the outbreak of war was captaining a fishing ketch, the *George Burrow*, owned by the Chambers family. When war broke out Thomas was at sea, not realizing that the war had started. He had by then been joined on the ketch by his son Thomas junior, but by April 1915 Thomas junior left to join the Royal Navy, leaving his father, who was considered too old for military service working as a fisherman, an occupation deemed to be vital to Britain's food supplies.

In a sad and ironic twist the *George Burrow* had passed the three Royal Navy vessels, HMS *Cressy*, HMS *Aboukir*, HMS *Hogue*, only a matter of hours before they were all sunk by the German submarine *U-9*. During the following weeks after they were sunk the *George Burrows* found the bodies of dead British sailors in their fishing nets.

In the spring of 1915 the *George Burrows* fell victim to the German U-boat strategy of sinking any and all Allied shipping. Soon after this the British authorities came up with a plan to use a flotilla of tiny fishing vessels that would be secretly armed with a 3-pounder guns, and used in a similar manner to the bigger Q-Ships.

On 15 August 1917 whilst on board HMS *Nelson* with the nine other crew members, one of whom was his son Thomas, sailing in the area known as Jim Howe Bank, the *Nelson* was engaged by an unknown German U-boat. In the exchange Thomas Crisp was mortally wounded and died in his son's arms, and although the rest of the crew took to their life boat and survived, Thomas Crisp's lifeless body went to a watery grave along with the wreck of the *Nelson*.

The British Government used the incident and Thomas Crisp's actions for propaganda purposes in an effort to raise public morale and increase the numbers of men enlisting in the armed forces. Prime Minister David Lloyd George made an impassioned speech in the House of Commons on 29 October 1917, emphasizing Crisp's personal sacrifice and devotion to duty.

For the actions that won him the Victoria Cross, his name is also commemorated on the bell at St Margaret's Church in Lowestoft, as well as the Roll of Honour, which is also displayed within the church. Thomas Crisp junior was awarded a Distinguished Service Medal for his actions during the same incident.

Officer found dead in Chatham Hotel

Albert Isaacs, who was originally from South Africa, was found dead in a hotel bedroom in the Brompton area of Chatham. He had been shot once but Police were not looking for anybody else in connection with his death, a strong indication that they viewed his unfortunate death as more likely to be a suicide rather than an act of murder by a third person.

At the time of his death Isaacs was a lieutenant in the 5th (Reserve) Battalion, Middlesex Regiment, which was a depot/training unit stationed at Chatham as part of the Thames and Medway Garrison. He is buried at the Chatham Memorial Synagogue Burial Ground.

Bombing of HMS *Pembroke* 3 September 1917

HMS *Pembroke* was part of the Royal Naval Barracks at Chatham, which at any given time always had a steady flow of men on site who were either undertaking their basic training or other naval related courses. It was an extremely busy location, with men and vehicles entering and leaving the camp regularly throughout any given day. Trying to keep a record of all of such comings and goings, must have been a logistical nightmare for those tasked with its management. Being able to confirm somebody's actual identity could not always have been easy.

In September 1917 there were even more naval ratings at HMS *Pembroke* than there usually would have been. Two months earlier, on 9 July, HMS *Vanguard* exploded and sank whilst at anchor in Scapa Flow, meaning that all of the recruits who had been due to join her crew had not left *Pembroke*. There had also been an outbreak of cerebrospinal meningitis at the barracks. To try and

Chatham Barracks lower entrance.

Chatham Naval Barracks.

prevent the virus from spreading, men had to be moved to other accommodation on the site. To this end the drill hall was used as additional sleeping quarters and so it was that on the evening of 3 September 1917 there were about 900 naval ratings crammed into the temporary drill hall accommodation. Most were asleep, whilst others were lying in their hammocks reading or chatting with friends and comrades. Little did they know that events elsewhere in Europe only a few hours beforehand, would, before the night was out, result in devastating consequences for some of them.

Chatham Barracks Parade Ground 'Stand Easy'.

At 9.30 the same evening five German Gotha G.V. bomber aircraft left their base at Gontrode in Belgium on what was to be their first night flight. The German high command had decided to change their attacks to night raids, due to the amount of aircraft they were losing during daytime raids. They were hoping that the cover of darkness would greatly reduce their losses of both aircraft and men. One of the aircraft had to return to Gontrode soon after take off due to engine trouble.

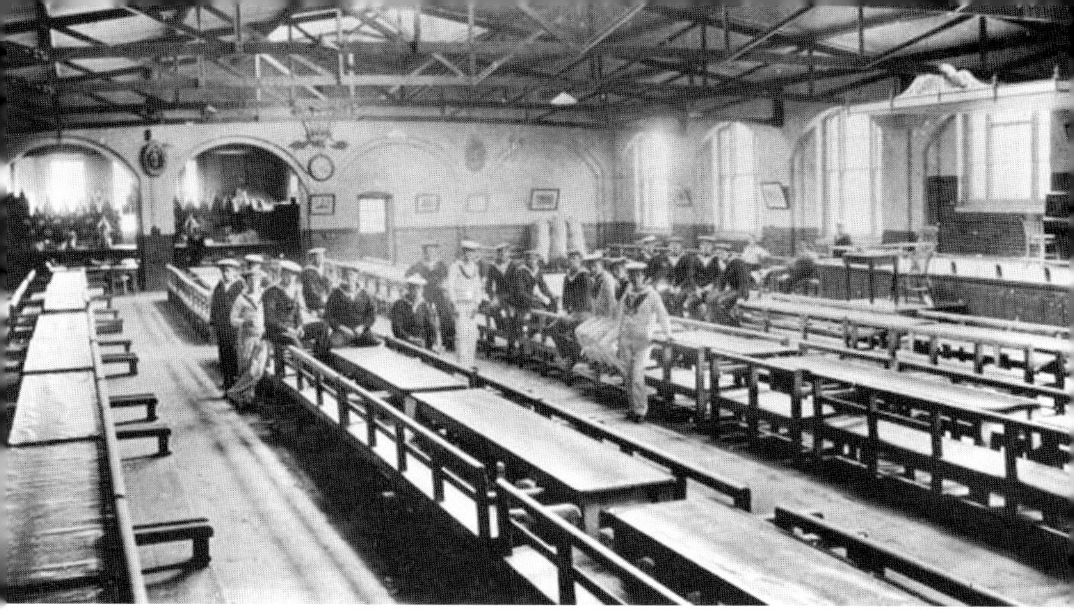

Chatham Naval Barracks canteen.

By around 11pm the four remaining Gotha bombers had reached the mouth of the River Medway as they passed over the Isle of Sheppey. The twists and turns of the river below were clearly visible to the crews, due to the towns of the Medway region, including Chatham, being lit up like Christmas trees. As such night raids had not been expected by the British authorities, there was no defensive strategy in place, even anti-aircraft guns not been manned.

During the raid the Gothas dropped a total of forty-six bombs on their unsuspecting victims below. The bombs were dropped all over Chatham and Gillingham, one scoring a direct hit on the drill hall at the barracks at HMS *Pembroke*. A section of the roof was made of glass and shattered as the bomb dropped through it, showering the sleeping sailors with large shards of glass, before it exploded on impact when it hit the floor of the drill hall. The clock on the wall stopped at 11:12pm, recording the exact time that the bomb dropped.

In the aftermath of the bombing, everybody helped with the many casualties, both officers and ratings alike. It would be 4pm the following day before the last of the dead and wounded had been fully accounted for. Many of the rescuers had remained there the entire time without a break.

Taken from 'The Chatham air-raid: events of Monday 3rd September 1917. The Great War, Chatham,' by R. Bedwell, the following were accounts of the incident as recorded by some of those who went to the assistance of those inside the drill hall after the bombing.

Ordinary Seaman Frederick W. Turpin, made notes of what he saw:

> *'It was a gruesome task. Everywhere we found bodies in a terribly mutilated condition. Some had arms and legs missing and some headless. The gathering up of dismembered limbs turned one sick. It was a terrible affair and the old sailors, who had been in several battles, said they would rather be in ten Jutlands or Heliogolands than go through another raid such as this.'*

Another who helped out on that fateful evening was a Mr E. Conk. He described what he saw:

> *'The raider dropped two bombs; one in the middle of the drill shed and one near the wall of the parade ground, just where the sailors were sleeping. I shall never forget that night, the lights fading and the clock stopping. We of the rescue party picking out bodies, and parts of bodies, from among glass and debris and placing them in bags, fetching out bodies in hammocks and laying them on a tarpaulin on the parade ground, you could not identify them. I carried one sailor to the sick bay who was riddled with shrapnel and had no clothes left on him. In the morning, to show that the officials could tell who was who, they had a general Pipe asking all the sailors of different messes if they could identify any of the lost: it was impossible in most cases. It was one of the most terrible nights I have ever known, the crying and the moaning of the dying men, who had ten minutes before been fast asleep.'*

Mr Gideon Gardiner who had been in the temporary morgue which had been set up with in the barracks gymnasium, gave the following account of what he had witnessed.

'Some had never woken up; apparently the shock appeared to have stopped their hearts. They were stretched out, white, gaunt, drawn faces, with eyes nearly bolted out of their heads. Others were greatly cut up, mangled, bleeding and some were blown limb from limb.'

The horror of war had arrived in Chatham that evening. For yet another English town, the war wasn't something that was taking place somewhere across the English Channel and further afield; for the people of Chatham it was now happening in their own back yard.

With all such events where the number of those who died is quite high, precise details on exact numbers of those who were killed can sometimes become confused, but the *Evening Despatch* dated 4 September 1917, recorded that 107 sailors had been killed and a further 86 had been injured. It also reported that there were six German aircraft that took part in the raid and that none of them were shot down.

The initial official report of the incident was exceedingly quick in its release. At 11:45pm, just half an hour after the bombing had taken place, Field Marshal Lord French, Commander-in-Chief of the Home Forces, released the following communique:

'Enemy aeroplanes passed the south-east coast at about 11pm, and dropped bombs at various places. No reports of casualties or damage have been received as yet. A number of our machines went up in pursuit.'

At 1pm the following day, 4 September, Lord French announced:

'Last night's air raid was carried out by about six enemy aeroplanes, which proceeded up the south bank of the Thames estuary as far as Chatham.

Bombs were dropped in the Isle of Thanet and in the Sheerness and Chatham area between 10.40 and 11.30pm.

There were no Army casualties, civilian casualties reported at present are one killed and six injured.

> *Material damage was slight. Our machines went up and anti-aircraft guns came into action, but without result.'*

Amazingly, even though he would have been in possession of the facts, he made absolutely no mention whatsoever of the devastation that had taken place at the drill hall at Pembroke Barracks in Chatham. Instead he left that to Secretary of the Admiralty, Sir Oswyn Murray, who made the very briefest of statements: *'In the course of the air raid last night the following casualties were caused to naval ratings; killed 107, wounded 86.'*

Between 3 September and 20 September 1917, thirty-eight men who had initially been wounded in the attack on the Drill Hall at Pembroke barracks, subsequently died of their injuries.

A sad coincidence of the night's events was that that particular Monday evening had been selected for anti-aircraft practice, and policemen were walking through the streets of Chatham, advising people not to be alarmed when they heard guns firing, just as the German Gothas began their attack.

A particularly sad story to come out of the evening's events concerned the Longley family who lived at 2 Church Terrace, Chatham. George Charles Longley, the head of the house and a draper's manager, went out leaving his wife, Mary, and his two daughters Lottie and Elsie. When George returned, his home was no more, having been completely demolished by one of the German bombs. The firemen had searched among the debris and found both of his daughters, who were bleeding from minor cuts to their faces. It was not until 11.30 the following morning, once all of the debris from the wrecked house had been removed, that Mary's body was discovered. George and the rest of his family were rehoused at 188 Thorold Road in Chatham.

At Mary's subsequent inquest, it was officially found that the cause of her death was, not surprisingly, *'due to the bomb falling from a hostile plane.'*

This was not the first tragedy that had befallen George Longley's family during the war. Six months earlier on 12 March 1917, his elder son, also George Charles Longley, aged 21, and a 1st Class Air Mechanic in the Royal Flying Corps, had died of his wounds whilst serving in France.

The *Evening Despatch* dated 4 September 1917 reported that 107 naval ratings had been killed along with one civilian. It also said that there were a further eighty-six naval ratings who had been wounded along with six civilians.

An article in Wikipedia states that it was estimated that ninety naval ratings died and another forty or so were so seriously injured that they were not expected to live. The same article also reported that a mass funeral took place on 6 September 1917 at the Woodlands cemetery at nearby Gillingham where ninety-eight men were buried who had been killed in the air raid on the drill-hall at Pembroke Barracks, and that a further twenty-five men were buried in later individual burials at other cemeteries. The main delay for most of these other burials was down to identification.

A check of the Commonwealth War Graves Commission website shows a total of eighty-six men who were buried at the cemetery, died on 3 September 1917. A further eleven men died on 4 September and a further man was shown to have died on 5 September, which makes a total of ninety-eight men who could have been buried at the cemetery on 6 September. All of these men were buried with full military honours.

Here is a list of the ninety-nine naval ratings who died on or after the evening of 3 September 1917 from the Drill Hall at HMS *Pembroke*, and who were subsequently buried at the Woodlands Cemetery in Gillingham in Kent.

John Thomas Abrey	James Anderson	Robert Anderson
Alfred Andrews	Harry Barker	Joseph Beha
George Joseph Bell	John Benson	Walter Beverley
Henry David Bird	George Boyd	Joseph Brightwell
Michael Brown	William Bullock	George Butler
Frederick Cable	George Cain	Albert Cairns
Thomas Carmichael	Charles Cash	Arthur Charlton

Reginald Clark	William Clark	John Clements
Albert Cluett	Knight Cooke	B. Corker
Francis Crocker	Thomas Cropley	William Curd
Victor Duckett	Raymond Ellis	Robert Ferrett
Alfred Finlay	Leonard Fish	Robert Franklin
Thomas Ginn	Albert Goddard	Horace Godden
William Godwin	Nathaniel Gooby	Charles Goodsell
John Green	George Gunn	John Hammond
Frederick Hartnall	Thomas Haville	Arthur Haxell
Archibald Hale	John Henderson	Henry Hill
Ernest Hoskins	Arthur Humphrey	Joseph Jackson
Sydney Jackson	H.O. Jones	Alexander Kennedy
Archibald Langridge	Frederick Lutitt	Frederick Upson
Charles Lemmon	W.A Littlewood	John Loose
Sidney Macey	Alexander MacGregor	John McGregor
Claud McIntyre	Neil Mackay	Alexander McLean
Gilbert McLoughlin	John McNish	John Major
Roland Mayes	Percy Moore	Jack Nicholson
William Nolan	William Osborne	Frederick Parker
Robert Peters	A. Purton	James Pye
F.W. Reyner	Sidney Seymour	Horace Sharp
William Shirley	George Shuttle	George Simpson
Robert Smith	William Smith	Alexander Sutherland
Arthur Voice	William Wakefield	Edmund Walsh
William Walton	James Warne	Henry Wate
G. Watson	Alfred Watts	Gregory Wootton

The following men were killed on either the evening of 3 September 1917, or subsequently died of their wounds and were buried at locations other than Woodlands Cemetery in Gillingham.

James Richards was killed on 3 September and is buried at the Liverpool (Ford) Roman Catholic Cemetery.

H.L. Bavister was killed on 3 September and is buried at the Mill Road Cemetery in Cambridge.

Frederick George Benmore was killed on 3 September and is buried at the East London Cemetery, Plaistow.

William George Berwick was killed on 3 September and is buried at Norwich Cemetery in Norfolk.

Charles Alfred Clarke was killed on 3 September and is buried at the Beccles Road Cemetery in Lowestoft.

Robert William Collett was killed on 3 September and is buried at the Islington Cemetery and Crematorium.

H.C. Cooney died of his wounds on 4 September and is buried at the Cowpen Cemetery in Blythe.

F.I. Diver who was killed on 3 September and is buried at the Thetford Cemetery in Norfolk.

J.K. Foreman died of his wounds on 4 September and is buried at the Trinity Cemetery in Aberdeen.

Alfred Gibbs died of his wounds on 4 September and is buried at the City of London & Tower Hamlets Cemetery.

George Gilbert died of his wounds on 4 September and is buried at the All Saints Church Cemetery in Newcastle-upon-Tyne.

A.E. Gladwell was killed on 3 September and is buried at the Clacton Cemetery.

S. Hadley was killed on 3 September and is buried at the Oxbridge Lane Cemetery at Stockton-on-Tees.

Stephen Percy Hare was killed on 3 September and is buried in St Clements Churchyard at Skegness.

William Dowsey Magog died of his wounds on 5 September and is buried at the Ryhope Road Cemetery in Sunderland.

N. Moore died of his wounds on 8 September and is buried in the St Kentigern's Roman Catholic Cemetery in Glasgow.

Alfred George Moss was killed on 3 September and is buried in the West Ham Cemetery.

Percy Walter Nicholls died of his wounds on 8 September and is buried at the East London Cemetery in Plaistow.

W.J. Payne was killed on 3 September and is buried at the Paddington Cemetery in London.

Bertie Pegram died of his wounds on 4 September and is buried in St Mary's Churchyard, Westmill.

George William Rae died of his wounds on 11 September and is buried at the Harton Cemetery in South Shields.

John Raven was killed on 3 September and is buried at the Gorleston Cemetery in Great Yarmouth.

S.G. Rigden was killed on 3 September and is buried at the Whitstable Cemetery.

William J. Steed was killed on 3 September and is buried at St Mary's Churchyard in Reculver.

William Edward Sullivan died of his wounds on 4 September and is buried in St Woolos Cemetery in Newport.

John William Venney was killed on 3 September and is buried at Cleethorpes Cemetery.

A. McD Westgarth died of his wounds on 4 September and is buried at the Kirkley Cemetery in Lowestoft.

Another sad story to come out of the bombing, whilst at the same time providing a good example of how difficult it can be to research such matters, was that of the Sharp brothers.

One of those killed during the attack on 3 September 1917, was 28-year-old, 1st Class Stoker Horace Stanley Sharp. He had been in the Royal Navy for five years and had served in operations in the Persian Gulf and Gallipoli. He had also been awarded the King's Medal for his service. On 5 September, the same day that news of Horace's death had reached his parents, Harry and Edith May Sharp, their other son, Harry Sharp had been admitted to hospital in France after having been shot in the back. So serious was the wound that he died in hospital later that day.

Harry had initially enlisted in the Army at the outbreak of the war when he was only 16 years of age, as a private (9797) in the Cambridgeshire Regiment, but when his true age was discovered in June 1915, he was discharged for being under military age and sent

Chatham Naval Barracks Officers' Quarters.

home to his family. But in January 1917, at the age of 18 and now old enough to be a soldier, he re-enlisted and became Private 228138 Sharp in the 1st (City of London) Battalion, Royal Fusiliers and he arrived in France the following month. This time there was to be no reprieve.

Numerous young men from across the country, who were not even old enough to join the Army, were nevertheless hell bent on doing so, and managed to hoodwink many a recruitment sergeant into letting them enlist, even though some of them obviously knew full well that those before them were under age, but with quotas to fill, it suited both parties for them to be accepted as soldiers.

Officer's death

Whilst a party of officers were undergoing a course on rifle grenade firing at Chatham on 3 October 1917, Lieutenant Cyril William Victor Lewis of the 6th Battalion, Middlesex Regiment, who was

Chatham Naval Barracks Main Gates.

Chatham Naval Barracks.

attached to the regiment's 1st Battalion, was accidently killed. He was struck on the back of his neck by a bolt head with considerable force, which resulted in serious injury. He was immediately conveyed to the nearby Chatham Military Hospital for treatment, but was pronounced dead on arrival. The inquest into Lieutenant Lewis's death, which was held on 6 October 1917, returned a verdict of 'accidental death'.

The evidence showed that a rifle used by another officer during grenade instruction exploded. Lieutenant Lewis, who was only ten yards away from his fellow officer at the time, was struck by a piece of the bolt head.

A subsequent examination of the rifle showed there was a flaw in its manufacture – sadly it was a tragedy just waiting to happen.

Chatham Barracks.

CHAPTER 5

1918
The Final Push

Although not a known fact in January 1918, the war was in its final year; people were tired and just wanted it over and done with, once and for all, and for what they saw as the senseless bloody killing, to stop. The initial 1914 feeling of euphoria and expectation of what was to come, the belief that they would quickly give the Germans a bit of a bloody nose, and be home in time for Christmas, had long since dissipated. Most families and communities across the United Kingdom had suffered or been directly affected by the war in one way or another.

In the final eleven months of the war, a total of 268,070 officers and men of the British and Dominion forces had lost their lives, with an estimated double that amount, wounded. But the deaths of soldiers did not stop when the war ended.

An amazing feature of the First World War was some young men's ability to make life even more difficult for themselves than it already was. If having been called up in to the Army to go and fight in the war wasn't a dangerous enough prospect, some wanted to complicate their lives even more. One such young man was 38-year-old Tom Wilkinson, (alias Tom Williams) a Sapper with the Royal Engineers stationed in Chatham.

On 21 May 1918 he found himself before the courts in Chatham facing a charge of not one, but two counts of bigamy. He had already allegedly gone through separate wedding ceremonies with four different women, and amazingly whilst still 'married' to wife number four, he had attempted to induce another woman from Chatham to become Mrs Williams the fifth.

Three of Wilkinson's four 'wives' were not only in court to listen to the proceedings, but they were all sitting next to one another. Whether they were there in a supportive capacity or in a combined act of three women scorned, is not recorded. At Kent Assizes he was convicted and sentenced to seven years penal servitude.

King George V visits Fort Pitt Military Hospital at Chatham

The king and queen, along with Princess Mary and Prince George, paid a visit to the officers and men who had been wounded during the naval operations at Zeebrugge and Ostend.

In one of the wards the king had a lengthy conversation with Lieutenant Franks who, although a patient on the ward, wasn't actually wounded during the operation, although he most definitely was a casualty of the day. Having taken part in the training and preparations for the attack, he developed appendicitis on the day before the actual operation, and therefore had to stay behind and undergo surgery. The king commiserated with him on his bad luck at having missed the mainly naval operation.

Staff at the hospital commented on the fact that Lieutenant Franks could hardly bear to hear about the raid without 'striking' himself in the stomach, so frustrated was he about missing it, although he was more than happy to make an exception in the king's case.

The King at the Docklands

King George V made yet another pre-arranged visit to both Chatham and Sheerness dockyards on 23 May 1918. This was his second visit of the month to Chatham. He received rousing ovations from the thousands present at both of his visits, where he met soldiers, sailors, war workers, ordinary members of the public and in particular, working women, whom he knew had provided a much needed service to keep the country's war effort going, while most of the men were off fighting in the war.

At Chatham, His Majesty chatted with many retired servicemen, whilst he passed through a veritable hive of different industries, all of which had some connection with the war. He witnessed the process for making torpedoes along with the construction for the latest type of submarine engines. The last part of his visit saw him chatting with the naval commanders of many of his fighting ships, some of which had splendid histories.

There was an interesting article in the newspapers dated Saturday 15 June 1918 concerning a 40-year-old senior officer in the Royal Navy – Lieutenant Commander Harry Macleod Fraser – who had an interesting military past.

On 31 July 1912 he became the commander of HMS *Boyne*, on 7 February 1913 commander of HMS *Swale* and in August 1914 commander of HMS *Doon*. By December 1914 he was the division leader of the 9th Destroyer Flotilla, which operated out of Chatham and included HMS *Trest*, HMS *Doon*, HMS *Waveney* and HMS *Moy*. On 16 December 1914 the flotilla was sent to patrol off Hartlepool on the north-east coast of the United Kingdom, on the same day that the northern town was attacked by two battle cruisers of the German Imperial Navy, the *Sieditz* and the *Moltke*, as well as an armoured cruiser, the *Blücher*.

The three German ships arrived off Hartlepool at around 0500 hours and were spotted about five miles to the north-east of the town. During the attack HMS *Doon* was damaged by German shell fire. One of her crew, Stoker 1st Class (SS/109383) James Fraser, was killed during the action, whilst another eleven members of the crew were wounded, and one of these, Able Seaman (177695) Harold Credland, died of his wounds the following day.

Shore batteries in Hartlepool returned fire, striking both the *Moltke* and the *Blücher* several times. This in turn brings us back to Lieutenant Commander Harry Macleod Fraser.

A case was heard before the Lord Chancellor, Viscount Haldane, sitting with Lord Atkinson, Lord Sumner and Lord Parmoor, in the House of Lords on 14 June 1918, which had been brought by Lieutenant Commander Harry Macleod Fraser, who was on the retired list of the Royal Navy, against Mr Arthur Balfour, who at the time had been the First Lord of the Admiralty.

Lieutenant Commander Fraser alleged that Mr Balfour had caused him to be imprisoned at Chatham Hospital and that there had been no lawful justification for him doing so. He further alleged that by being so forcibly detained, he had suffered unspecified 'damage'. One can only assume that this means in a mental capacity. The allegations didn't stop there. Fraser also claimed that Balfour issued an order which in effect ended his naval career and forced him in to an early retirement which he most certainly did not want.

Detectives v Bluejackets

On 26 September 1918, detectives from Chatham Police chased after three bluejackets (sailors) who were all absentees and on the run after having broken into the YMCA hut at Chatham, and made off with the safe, which contained £23 in cash, postal orders and stamps. The safe was eventually found some three miles away. It had been opened and its contents removed.

So determined were the detectives to arrest those responsible that they carried on the chase for several miles, across fields and down lanes. It was eventually discovered that the three men responsible had been arrested and detained at nearby Malling. The Chatham detectives brought the men back to Chatham to be interviewed about the burglary.

German U-boat 122

The German word *Unterseeboot* which has long since been shortened to the universally recognisable U-boat, literally translates in English to 'undersea boat', and during both world wars was the scourge of Allied shipping.

Remarkably, at the beginning of the First World War, Germany had just twenty-eight U-boats in its maritime fleet. By the end of

UB-122.

the war German industry had gone into overdrive and had managed to build a total of 360 sea-worthy submarines, which means that one submarine was built nearly every four days throughout the entire war. Of these 178 were sunk by the Allies, or were otherwise lost, which resulted in the loss of some 5,000 German sailors.

The submarine *UB-122* was a late addition to the German Imperial Navy, having only been launched on 2 February 1918 and commissioned at Bremen on 4 March 1918, under the command of Oberleutnant zur See Alexander Magnus, who, though aged only 25, had already been awarded the Iron Cross, both 1st and 2nd Class. *UB-122* only carried out two patrols and on both occasions she did not see any action. She was surrendered to the British authorities on 24 November 1918, in line with the conditions of the Armistice. She would have had a complement of three officers and thirty-one crewmen.

After the Armistice and Germany's surrender, about one hundred of her submarines were sailed by their crews to Harwich. Some time later, possibly as late as 1921, and after parts of the vessels such as their engines were removed, most of them were destined to be scrapped. *UB-122* is believed to have broken her tow line en route to her final destination, and was washed into the River Medway. At low tide the remains of what is believed to have been this vessel, can still be clearly seen on a remote part of the Kent marshes, having resurfaced some ninety-two years after she disappeared. A few were maintained as submarines and provided to Allied navies.

Kent Australians who fell in The Great War

Amateur Historian Andrew Bratley, who was born in Maidstone, Kent, but who now lives in Perth, Western Australia, has researched those men who were born in Kent, but who served in and subsequently died whilst fighting with the Australian Imperial Force (AIF). He discovered 223 men who had lost their lives in this way; eighteen of them were from the areas of Chatham, Gillingham and Rochester. With Andrew's kind permission this part of his research is included below.

Private Thomas Ronald **Biggs** (3357) was a 20-year-old private in the 59th Battalion AIF when he was killed in action on 25 April 1918. He is buried at the Adelaide Cemetery, in the Somme region of France.

His parents, Thomas and Mary Biggs, had previously lived at 22 Fox Street, Gillingham and by profession Thomas Senior was a painter and decorator. Thomas junior was the eldest of three brothers; Reginald and Frederick were both too young to have served in the war.

It is not clear when and why Thomas left England to live in Australia, but it was after 1911 as he appears on the UK Census of that year, when he was only 13 years of age.

Private William Thomas **Buckley** (6957) was a 23-year-old private in the 4th Battalion AIF. He was born on 27 April 1895 at Gillingham and lived with his parents, William and Alice Buckley, along with his two elder sisters, Margurette, Ethel and his elder brother Alfred, at 105 Kingswood Road, Gillingham. It is not known if Alfred served his country during the war, although he was old enough to have done so.

William was killed in action at Démuin, France on 13 September 1918. He is buried in the Roisel Communal Cemetery on the Somme.

Battery Sergeant Major Douglas Frederick **Handford** (1601), of the 7th Battery, Australian Field Artillery, was killed in action at Gallipoli on 6 August 1915. He is buried at the Shell Green Cemetery in Turkey.

His sister, Nellie Medhurst, lived at 52 Richmond Road, Gillingham. Douglas was a man of Kent, having been born at Dover. In his will, he left £111 18s to his wife, Eliza Handford, who was living at Drillham in Queensland.

According to 1901 Census, when Douglas was only 15 years of age, he had already enlisted in the Army and was a boy soldier in the Royal Garrison Artillery, stationed at Dover Castle. By the time of the 1911 Census, Douglas was still with the Royal Garrison Artillery stationed in India, but had now reached the rank of corporal, and been in the Army for ten years. He had a sister, Hellie, and three brothers: Herbert who was older than him and Sidney and Horace, who were both younger. I could find no sign of Sidney having served in the military during the First World War, but both Herbert and Horace did. Like Douglas, Herbert also served in the Royal Garrison Artillery, as a battery sergeant (27619) with the 32nd Siege Battery. He served in Mesopotamia during the war and on 22 September 1919 his award of the Meritorious Service Medal was gazetted. Horace served as a corporal (33742) in the Royal Artillery (Royal Horse Artillery and Royal Field Artillery). Both Herbert and Horace survived the war.

Private George **Harrad** (5033), who was born in Gillingham, was in the 50th Battalion AIF when he was killed in action on 13 August 1918 at Bray. He was 41 years of age at the time of his death and his name is commemorated on the Villers Bretonneux Memorial on the Somme.

George's mother, Emma Harrad, lived at 160 Napier Gardens,

Gillingham, and his younger brother and sister, who by the time of his death had both married and left home, still lived in the town as well.

Private Trevor **James** (2490) of the 16th Battalion AIF, was killed in action at Lone Pine in Turkey on 7 August 1915. He was born in Rochester, Kent in 1892.

Private Arthur Henry **Jeffery** (4069) was 20 years of age and serving in the 32nd Battalion AIF at the time of his death on 6 May 1918, not from wounds received in battle, but from injuries he received whilst taking part in a training exercise. He is buried at the Pernois British Cemetery which is situated on the Somme.

Lance Corporal William Thomas **Jeffery** (1052) was Arthur's brother serving in the 28th Battalion AIF. Having taken part in the failed Gallipoli campaign, he was subsequently killed in action near Pozières, France on 29 July 1916. He has no known grave and his name is commemorated on the Villers-Bretonneux Memorial, in the Somme region of France.

Arthur and William's parents, William (senior) and Ellen Jeffery, lived at 3 Prentice Street, Strood, Rochester, Kent.

The Villers-Bretonneux Memorial is an important edifice for Australians, as it is their national memorial and was erected in

Villers-Bretonneux Memorial, France. (Commonwealth War Graves Commission.)

memory of not only those men from Australia who were killed, but to all of those men who fought in either Belgium or France at any time during the course of the Great War.

The memorial, which records the names of over 10,000 Australian military personnel, was unveiled by King George Vl on 22 July 1938, and forms part of the Villers-Bretonneux Military Cemetery.

William and his regiment had previously served with Allied forces during the failed Gallipoli campaign, before they were subsequently redeployed to France.

William Arthur Jeffery.

Private George **Osborn** (2135) of the 16th Battalion AIF died of his wounds on 14 August 1915. A Kent man who was born in Chatham, he was buried at the Alexandria (Chatby) Military and War Memorial Cemetery, in Egypt.

Lance Corporal Frederick William **Reed** (177) served with the 22nd Battalion, Australian Light Horse, which was part of the

Frederick William Reed, third form right with head bowed August 1914.

Australian XXII Corps. He was 32 years of age when he was killed during a defensive action on 11 April 1918 during fierce fighting with German forces in around the area of Hooge Chateau, which resulted in the Germans regaining the area, which they held until 28 September. Frederick is buried at the Hooge Crater Cemetery, Belgium. His widow lived at 22 College Avenue, in Gillingham.

He was either not quite ready when the above photograph was taken or for some reason he didn't want to have his picture taken.

Private William John **Richards** (580) aged 27 of the 13th Battalion AIF, died of his wounds on 9 July 1917. He is buried at the Trois Arbres Cemetery, Steenwerck, in the Nord region of France.

The village had been held by the Allies throughout the war and in July 1916 had become home to the 2nd Australian Casualty Clearing Station, before being lost to the Germans on 10 April 1918. William's parents lived at St James Street in Gillingham.

Private David **Smith** (726) of the 37th Battalion AIF, was aged 20 when he was killed in action on 19 July 1918, in no man's land, just west of Hamel, on the Somme. He was buried at the Crucifix Corner Cemetery, at Villers-Bretonneux. His parents, William and Fanny Smith, lived in the High Halstow area of Rochester.

Private Charles **Woolnough** (6108), who was born in Rochester, was 35 years of age and serving in the 3rd Battalion, Australian Machine Gun Corps, when he died on 21 March 1919 of broncho-pneumonia, whilst still serving in France.

Prior to the war he had served as both a fireman on the River Thames and the River Medway, and as a barge captain for the Portland Cement Manufacturers.

One of Charles's four brothers, Thomas Henry Woolnough, also fought with the Australian Forces. He was a sergeant (3022) in the 28th Battalion AIF and was awarded the Military Medal for bravery which was gazetted on 21 October 1918 (p12423). On most occasions there was no accompanying citation for the award of the Military Medal.

Private Nathaniel **Pritchard** (3455) was aged 33 and serving in the 55th Battalion AIF, when he was killed in action on 19 October 1917, near Polygon Wood in Belgium. His grave is at the Aeroplane Cemetery, in the West-Vlaanderen region of Belgium. The cemetery was originally called the New Cemetery Frezenberg when it was begun in August 1917, but it was changed two months later due to an aeroplane which crashed nearby. Until 31 July 1917 the location of the cemetery was actually part of no man's land between Allied and German trench lines.

Nathaniel was born in Chatham in 1885 and by 1901 he was a shoemaker by profession, living with his mother, Alice, elder sister, Minnie, and a boarder by the name of Benjamin Cove, in Camberwell, London. Ten years later he was living at the Hollesley Bay Labour Colony, in Woodbridge, Suffolk, where he was working as a rigger's mate.

Private Ernest **Tanner** (7147), who was born in Chatham in 1898, was with the 28th Battalion AIF, when he was killed in action on 10 June 1918, during fighting at Morlancourt on the Somme. He is buried in the Beacon Cemetery on the outskirts of the French village of Sailly-Laurette, an area that did not see any fighting until 26 March 1918.

Corporal William Joseph **Branch** was born at Chatham on 16 November 1883. Between 15 July 1901 and 15 November 1913, he was an able seaman in the Royal Navy. After the outbreak of the war, he decided to re-enlist but not in the Navy, this time he chose the Army. He became a corporal (1344) in the 45th Battalion AIF. He died wounds on 19 October 1917 and is buried at the Ypres Reservoir Cemetery in Belgium.

One of William's brothers, George, who was in the Mercantile Marine, deserted from the Royal Mail Steamer *Moldavia* when it docked in Sydney, Australia, on 16 July 1909. A warrant was issued for his arrest by the Water Police Bench.

Private Henry Thomas **Allery** (396) of the 11th Battalion AIF, died of his wounds on 5 July 1915. Born in Deptford, London in 1880, he was wounded during fighting at Gallipoli. Between 7 March 1899 and 6 March 1911, Henry had served as a private (5887) in both the 1st and 2nd Battalions, East Kent Regiment (The Buffs), having enlisted at the age of 19, on 7 March 1899 at Dover. His twelve years of Army life had seen him twice serve in South Africa, the latter occasion being during the Second Boer War of 1899–1902, as well as a period of two years when he was stationed in Hong Kong.

His parents, William Henry and Julia Allery, lived at 29 Gardeners Court, Chatham and prior to that at 19 Union Street in Dover, although his mother, Julia, died in 1897. He had an elder sister whose name was also Julia, whilst his brother, William, served as a private (1249) with the 1st Battalion, East Surrey Regiment and first arrived in France on 18 February 1915. After having been on the Western Front for only two months, he was reported as missing in action on 20 April 1915. His body was never found and it was officially presumed that he had been killed on that day. At the time of his death, he was 46 years of age.

Private Henry Francis Charles **Turner** (820) of the 9th Battalion, AIF was killed in action whilst fighting at Gallipoli on 25 April 1915 aged 21. His name is commemorated on the Lone Pine Memorial in Turkey.

Henry had only arrived in Australia the previous year having left London a month before the outbreak of war, on 3 July 1914, on board the SS *Ovieto*, bound for Brisbane. His parents, Henry and Jessie Turner, lived at 263 Castle Road, Chatham, along with his two younger sisters, May and Jessie.

Barrage Balloon Station – Chatham

During the last years of the First World War, Britain began

deploying barrage balloons as part of the defensive strategy to protect many prominent locations, the City of London being the main one. The Royal Docks at Chatham were another such location that had been identified as a potential target for German aircraft. Used in conjunction with anti-aircraft units as well as search light sections, they proved to be a pretty effective deterrent, although not totally foolproof.

The balloons were connected to points on the ground with lengths of cable, which allowed for the different heights they could be set at, usually between 7,500 and 10,000 feet. This meant that attacking German aircraft had to stay above this height, as flying under the balloons meant they ran the very real risk of crashing into the steel cables and almost certain death.

The idea of barrage balloons was conceived by Major General Ashmore, the commanding officer of the London Air Defences who, it was said, came up with his quirky invention the morning after the first German Gotha night attack had taken place over London in the first week of September 1917. The first barrage balloon was in fact a borrowed observation balloon, the type that had been in use in France throughout the war.

Aircraft factory Rochester

After their first flight in a coal gas filled balloon, in 1897, the Short brothers, Oswald and Eustace, continued to experiment in the arena of flight, eventually founding their own aviation company in 1908, making it the first such company in the world. In 1913, Mr Willis, who was a local councillor, sold an 8.4 acre plot of land to the Short brothers at Borstal near Rochester, so allowing them to build premises for the production of seaplanes; but it would be another two years before the facility was completed and became known as the Seaplane Works.

At the time flight was still in its infancy, with the first recorded powered flight only having been achieved in 1903 by the Wright brothers. It would be a further six years before improvements had advanced sufficiently for the French pilot, Louis Blériot, to be able to fly across the English Channel in 1909. By the outbreak of the First World War in August 1914, flying was still in its comparative infancy, and not surprisingly the life expectancy of a young trainee pilot was not good. In 1914 more British pilots had a higher chance of dying whilst undergoing training than they did when engaged in combat.

In 1918 this premise was confirmed when William H. Wilmer wrote that out of every one hundred British military pilot deaths during the initial year of the First World War, ninety resulted from individual deficiencies, sixty of these being because of physical defects, eight from aircraft defects, and only two as a result of enemy action.

Initially British authorities and senior military personnel were slow to embrace the full potential of flight and the aircraft which they had at their disposal, instead only seeing something that was useful for intelligence gathering, reconnaissance and aerial photography. By comparison with today's standards, attitudes towards the personal wellbeing of a pilot during the early years of the First World War was absolutely staggering. Pilots were not allowed the safety precaution of a parachute, even though they were readily available. The thinking behind this decision was the belief by certain senior Army officers that the carrying of a parachute might 'dilute the fighting spirit of pilots', this despite the knowledge that if an aircraft caught fire in flight the only options a stricken pilot had were either to sit in the cockpit of his doomed aircraft and wait to be overcome by flames, or to jump to a certain death – not much of a choice either way for a brave young man.

Chatham's Wartime Regiments

The Kent Fortress Royal Engineers wartime connection with Chatham is well documented, but there were other military units stationed in the town during the course of the war. The Royal West Kent Regiment was represented by F and G Companies of the 1st/5th Battalion (Territorial Force).

The Middlesex Regiment had both the 5th and 6th Reserve

Battalions, which formed part of the Thames and Medway Garrison. At the outbreak of the war both were stationed at Mill Hill in London, but on mobilization, the 5th Battalion moved to Rochester and the 6th to Gillingham. In November 1915 the 6th moved on to Chatham where they remained for the rest of the war. The 5th also moved to Chatham, but not until March 1916; by 1917 they were in Gillingham, where they stayed for the rest of the war.

The Middlesex Regiment had a long and distinguished history which included being part of Wellington's Army during the Peninsular Wars. They also had the distinction of being the first Regiment of the British Army to arrive in France during the First World War, with two companies having arrived on 11 August, a further two companies the following day and the remainder of the regiment arriving a week later on the 19th.

Cooks of the 6th Battalion, Middlesex Regiment at the North Cookhouse, Chatham Barracks.

CHAPTER 6

Some Who Returned

Those who survived the war and returned home to their friends and families are quite often, albeit unintentionally, forgotten about historically. Unless they were awarded a medal for bravery, such as the Victoria Cross, little is known or recorded about their actions and exploits during the war. It is those who are killed in action, die of their wounds or succumb to illness or disease that history remembers on a Roll of Honour or a War Memorial, found in most towns and villages up and down the country.

The British Army Pension records that cover the period of the First World War, show that a total of 329 men who were born in Chatham, but who were not necessarily living in the town before or after the war, were awarded an Army pension, which indicates that they survived. The same records show that there were forty men living in Chatham after the war who were also in receipt of an Army pension, although this doesn't mean that they were necessarily born in the town. It is this last group that I want to look at in more detail.

The surviving British Army Service records and the British Army Pension records are also known as the Burnt Documents, due to the fact that over two thirds of 6.5 million records were destroyed during the Second World War, as a result of a German bombing raid on the City of London in September 1940, when an incendiary bomb set fire to the War Office Record Store in Arnside Street, London. The records which survived became known as the Burnt

Documents. This means that the figures quoted about the number of men who survived and returned home cannot be absolutely exact.

Besides those who died for their country and those who were wounded, there were others whose military service came to an abrupt end because of illness, ailments and disease, some of whom undoubtedly hid their problems from medical examiners only for them to come to light at a later time. Some of these conditions would appear to have been quite obvious, highlighting the pressure on recruitment centres to get as many men signed up as possible

William John **Adams** was born in Chatham in 1898 and after the war was living at 20 Halcombe Road, Chatham. This was the address of his parents, Frederick and Mary Ann Adams. William had three brothers and five sisters.

He was originally allocated to the Southampton Regiment as private 26979. Having attested on 7 June 1916 he was immediately placed on the Army Reserve, before being mobilized the following year on 18 April 1917 and posted to the Army Veterinary Corps where he ended up as a sergeant. He served in Russia after the end of the war between 6 September 1919 and 28 June 1920. From there he was sent to Constantinople for three months between 29 June and 28 September 1920.

He was awarded the Russian Order of Saint Stanislaus on 20 November 1920. The order reflects chivalry in its purest form, which is 'people helping people'. It was established on 8 May 1765 by King Stanislas of Poland, Augustus Poniatowski, to honour the patron of that country, but it became an Order of the Russian Empire after Poland was united into the Russian Empire after the Polish – Russian war of 1830–1831.

I could not find the reason why William had been given the award, but interestingly enough, with the Russian Revolution and the abdication of King Nicholas ll in March 1917, the Order of Saint Stanislaus fell into abeyance and was not fully re-established until 9 June 1979, so it remains something of a mystery as to why he was given it in 1920.

He was finally demobbed on 1 December 1920 although for the last sixty-one days of his service, from 1 October 1920, he had been on furlough.

Alfred **Arnold** was born in 1882 and was a married man. With his wife Mary, he had eight children, earning his money by working two jobs, as a green grocer and a coal merchant. He originally enlisted in the Royal Engineers as a private (210634) but later transferred, and served with the 9th (Depot) Battalion, The Rifle Brigade.

Having been conscripted at Maidstone on 2 March 1916, he was eventually called up on 29 November 1916. He served in France as part of the British Expeditionary Force between 11 May 1917 and 14 March 1918, a total of 308 days, after which time he returned home on leave.

Alfred's story is a very interesting one. He was medically discharged from the Army for being no longer physically fit for war service

On his first day on leave back home in Chatham, Alfred decided upon some DIY, which resulted in his slicing off three of the fingers on his right hand in a slicing machine. He was admitted to the Central Medical Hospital at Fort Pitt, Chatham, where he stayed until 21 March 1918, when he was moved to the Howard de Walden Hospital in Maidstone for further treatment, where he stayed until 19 April 1918.

An Army medical report written about Alfred whilst he was being treated at Fort Pitt, included the following:

> *'First came into Fort Pitt with 1st, 2nd, and 3rd fingers right hand severed down to the 2nd joint. Said he cut them off in a cutting machine while on leave. He had been in France the preceding 11 months. No mishaps.'*

The fourth finger of the same hand had also been badly damaged in the incident, but it was not possible for the finger to be removed.

The reason given was illegible on the report.

After the war he was living at 286 Chatham Hill, Chatham, in the same street as his parents who lived at 252 Chatham Hill.

William **Barnard** was born in 1876 and was a labourer by trade. He enlisted in the Army on 10 December 1915 but wasn't mobilized until 28 February 1916 when he became Private G/12359 in the 3rd Battalion the Queen's Own (Royal West Kent Regiment).

William's eyesight had begun to fail in 1912, although he had still been passed as being fit when he had his Army medical three years later. Whilst he was serving in France he injured his right foot when a trench board fell on it. He had three spells in hospital, the first of which was at the Fort Pitt Military Hospital in Chatham, when he was treated for osteoarthritis, between 9 May and 7 June 1916. He was then transferred to the West Hall Hospital in Tunbridge Wells, where he stayed until 26 June 1916 for a continuation of the same treatment. On 29 January 1917 he was admitted to the City of London Military Hospital, 42 Clifton Road, Clapton for treatment for an enlarged metatarsal. He was a patient there until 13 February 1917.

William Barnard was discharged from the Army as no longer being physically fit enough for war service, on 29 May 1917 at Hounslow. He was 42 years of age. After the war he was living at 30 Bush Street, Chatham.

Sidney Robert **Beaumont** was born in 1897 and after the war was living at 39 Eva Road, Chatham. He served with the 84th Training Reserve Battery as Private 5/59669. He was called up on 21 July 1917 and was discharged from the Army as no longer fit for war service on 8 October 1917 at York, still only 20 years of age, having served for a total of 110 days. A medical report which forms part of his British Army Pension papers included the following remarks: *'This man states that his feet have caused him pain when walking since infancy. He now complains of inability to march when out training.'*

On the strength of this he was found to be permanently unfit for war service and was medically discharged from the Army. He did however have to present himself for a medical re-examination one year after his discharge, under the conditions of the Military Services (Review of Exemptions) Act 1917. He did what was required of him and it was deemed that there was no change in his medical condition. In essence he was suffering with flat feet.

Robert **Beckett** was born in 1876 and after the war was living at 23 Best Road, Chatham. He served as Private 154350 in the 5th Battalion, Labour Corps. He enlisted in the Army on 10 December 1915 at Chatham, was mobilized on 27 October 1916 and discharged on 2 October 1917 at Nottingham. When a soldier was deemed to be no longer physically fit enough to undertake war service, he was medically discharged under Paragraph 392 (xv1) of King's Regulations.

The reason why Robert was medically discharged was because of a hernia which had originated some fourteen years previously. His medical form also includes the fact that the hernia had not been aggravated by 'ordinary military service'. This was a slightly strange statement as Robert had already served in the Army for a year when he was discharged, and if the hernia issue, which had not been a problem when he enlisted and during his initial training, was the reason, then surely the hernia must have been aggravated since he had joined the Army.

His medical record doesn't show what actually led to his hernia suddenly becoming so bad that he had to be discharged from the Army, but it was a medical board chaired by Captain R. Adams, of the Royal Army Medical Corps, who gave the authority for Robert's discharge. The hearing was held at the 1st Eastern General Hospital in Cambridge on 17 August 1917, where Robert had been a patient between 2 June and 18 August 1917.

John **Brady** has a truly remarkable story even though he didn't actually serve during the First World War, but he was an Army pensioner living in Chatham and as such, he deserves to be included in this chapter of the book. He was born in Warrington, Lancashire in 1867 but by the end of the war he was living at 63 Beaconsfield Road in Chatham.

He initially enlisted in the 8th Battalion, The Lancashire Regiment as Private 789 in 1882, when he was just 16 years of age, eventually rising to the rank of band master, warrant officer (9260) in C Company, 4th Battalion, The Rifle Brigade, to which he transferred on 1 August 1902, at which time he was permitted to continue in the service beyond twenty-one years for a period of five years until 2 October 1913, which took him past his thirtieth year in the Army. He had served in South Africa between 26 June 1884 and 9 February 1887. He was also stationed in Gibraltar, Malta, Egypt and India. During his time with the Rifle Brigade he was not separated from his wife, Francis Gertrude Brady, as she also worked for the Corps and moved around the different locations with him.

He was eventually discharged on 17 January 1913 at Gosport, having served for a remarkable 30 years and 108 days. He was just three months away from his forty-seventh birthday. Not surprisingly, having accumulated such a length of service, he had been awarded his Long Service and Good Conduct Medal.

Frank **Brown** was born in Barking, Essex in 1890. He was a married man, having married Eva Louisa Trussell on 31 August 1914 at Barking Parish Church.

He attested on 4 December 1915 at Windsor and was placed in the Army Reserve, but not mobilized until 13 April 1917 when he became Private 2753 in the Reserve Household Battalion. He was nearly 26 years old and by profession he was a school teacher. On 14 July 1917 he arrived at Le Havre in France, having sailed from Southampton. Whilst there he transferred to the 2nd Battalion, Grenadier Guards as private 34634, where he remained until 9 January 1919.

His time in France had also seen him requiring medical treatment on more than one occasion, although it is not clear from his Army Medical Record what injuries or illnesses he had sustained.

On 9 December 1917 he was admitted to the 103rd Field Ambulance, a front line medical unit and part of the 34th Division. Three days later he was admitted to No.8 Casualty Clearing Station which had been situated in Bailleul since 21 November 1914. He was only there for two days before being transferred to No.7 Canadian General Hospital at Etaples.

On 1 February 1918 he was admitted to the General Hospital at Trouville. Later that year on 27 September 1918, Frank was wounded in action and treated by the 2nd Field Ambulance before being moved later the same day to the 4th Casualty Clearing Station, at Pont-Remy.

He was demobilized on 17 February 1919 and placed on the Army Reserve, before being fully demobilized on 21 March 1920. After the war he lived at 40 Ewart Road, Chatham.

Albert **Castle** was born in 1887. During the war he served with the 4th Battalion, East Surrey Regiment, as Private 32962. He was medically discharged from the Army on 9 June 1917 at Hounslow, having served for one year and 206 days, as no longer physically fit for war service due to chronic bronchitis and asthma. These were ailments which Albert had suffered from since his infancy, and although they had not come about as a result of his war service, they had been aggravated by it, especially when exposed to the cold and wet. He was awarded an Army pension of 13/9 per week, payable for 26 weeks.

After the war his address was 12 Edinburgh Road, Chatham.

Henry John **Chapell** was born in 1900 at Faversham in Kent, the eldest son of Jane and Henry Chapell. He was conscripted into the Army on 22 September 1917 but was not mobilized until 6 June 1918 at Caterham. Less than three weeks after having begun his Army life, he was admitted to Bermondsey Military Hospital, Ladywell in south-east London, suffering with flu. So bad were his symptoms that he spent thirteen days in hospital.

Although he had said on his attestation form that he wished to be considered for service with the Royal West Kent Regiment, he was allocated to serve with the 14th Battalion, Grenadier Guards as Guardsman 34663, and was finally discharged on 31 March 1920. After the war Henry lived at 7 First Avenue, Luton, Chatham.

Harry **Cheeseman** was born in 1891 and before the war he was a farmer in Chatham. He was 27 years old when he joined the Royal Defence Corps as Private 74084, in the 53rd Provost Company, on 12 September 1917 at Maidstone.

On 12 May 1914, three months before the outbreak of the war, he fractured his tibia when a horse fell on him which resulted in his leg being in plaster for four months and having to stay in hospital on two separate occasions. Despite this he was still able to enlist. Whether he was just being brave and covering up his injury or it was aggravated during his initial training, is not clear.

Harry went before a medical board on 3 June 1918 at Kings Lynn, which was chaired by Captain J.R. Kingdom, RAMC. It was noted that the tibia of his right leg was 'much swollen' and that he could only walk on the leg with difficulty and pain, caused no doubt by the visible thickening of the bone of the right tibia.

He was discharged on 4 July 1918 in London as no longer fit for war service, and was awarded a pension of 8s 3d for a total of eighteen weeks. His subsequent disability was stated to be 30 per cent permanent, and his pension records show that in the opinion of the medical board, his injuries were neither due to, nor aggravated by, his war service, yet he was still awarded an Army pension. Consequently Harry was awarded a Silver War Badge, which signified to others that the wearer of such a badge had been wounded whilst serving their country. The number of Harry's badge was 474589; it was a personal issue, and if lost could not be re-issued or replaced.

After the war he lived at a bungalow called 'The Mount' in Chatham.

Richard **Cherry** was born in 1880 and, after enlisting at Chatham on 4 December 1915, he served with the Queen's Own (Royal West Kent Regiment) as Private 12807, but he wasn't mobilized at Maidstone until 25 March 1916 when he was 35 years of age.

His medical notes, which were completed at the time of his initial enlistment, showed that he suffered with bad teeth.

On 14 April 1916, just three weeks after he had been called up, he was transferred to B Company, 2nd/4th Battalion, Norfolk Regiment, also as a private (6476) and only two months after that on 16 May 1916, he was discharged from the Army as no longer physically fit for war service, having served for just eighty-four days. The submitted application for his discharge as a recruit not likely to become an efficient soldier, was heard before a medical board held at Bury St Edmunds on 2 June 1916.

The reason for his medical discharge makes for interesting reading and shows how the use of the English language has changed somewhat over the years:

> *'Mental deficiency. He cannot read or write and is quite unable to learn his drill. Teeth are very defective and he is suffering from the effects of pyorrhoea alveolaris. Not the result of military service.'*

It has to be said that the levels of literacy, not just in England or throughout the United Kingdom, but across Europe and throughout the Americas, were not as high as they are today, but were probably as high as they had ever been up to that point in time. Many communities throughout the country were rural and village based, so maybe in some of these localities, levels of literacy were not as high as they were in some of the bigger towns and cities.

Immediately before, as well as after the war, he lived at 47 Dukes Cottages, Chatham, working as a farm labourer.

William George **Coster** was born in 1887. He was a painter and decorator by trade, but he put that on hold to go off and serve his king and country, which he did when he enlisted in the Army on 15 December 1915 at Chatham, just a month short of his thirty-eighth birthday. He was not mobilised until 17 June 1916 at Maidstone when he became Private 13046 in the 3rd Battalion, Royal Sussex Regiment.

He was a married man, having wed Rossetta Manning on 16 February 1903 at St Paul's Parish Church in Chatham. They had two daughters, Violet and Mariam, who were born in 1910 and 1912 respectively.

William was medically discharged from the Army on 17 July 1916 for not being likely to become an efficient soldier, due to heart related problems, after having served for a total of 189 days. Whilst undertaking basic drill instruction, William had complained of breathlessness, sickness, and pain in his chest, causing him to 'fall out'. On the last occasion this took place, he was examined by a medical officer from the Royal Army Medical Corps, who deemed him to be in a dangerous condition, adding at the end of the report that this was not due to military service, although it would be almost inconceivable that William's illness had not been affected by his war time service.

James **Cramp** was born in 1896. He served with the Grenadier Guards as Guardsman 24615, enlisting on 16 November 1915 at Chatham, when he was just 19 years old.

On his Army service record there was an entry which had been stamped, 'MISSING' which was dated 19 November 1916, and another immediately underneath it which said, 'Next of Kin Notified' on 1 December 1916. Both of these entries were subsequently crossed through, the inference being that somebody had made a clerical error.

He served in France with the British Expeditionary Force in the 2nd Battalion, Grenadier Guards, between 13 August 1916 and 25 December 1916, before returning home, where he was stationed for a year. Whilst in France, he transferred to the 7th (Guards) Entrenching Battalion on 23 August 1916, before moving on to the

Sanitary Section Guards Division on 23 November 1916. He was with them for just over a week before he re-joined the 2nd Battalion on 1 December, but was only with them for a week before he was moved yet again, this time being attached to the 1st Guards Brigade. No sooner had he arrived there than he was off again, this time to the Field Ambulance, No.14 Casualty Clearing Station, on 9 December 1916.

With Christmas fast approaching, he was transferred to No.3 Stationary Hospital in Rouen, but he was only there for three days before he returned to the UK on board HS *Dunluce Castle*, suffering with a minor bout of trench foot. On his arrival he was transferred to the 5th (Reserve) Battalion, Grenadier Guards. Poor old James had been transferred and attached to so many different sections during his time in France, he must have been dizzy, wondering whether he was coming or going.

Life in France wasn't just one big round of transfers for James, he was also disciplined on 10 September 1916 on charges of, *'when on active service, using obscene language in the hut'* and for *'speaking inappropriately to an NCO.'* He was found guilty on both charges and punished with seven days on field rations with no tea.

On 30 December 1917, he once again returned to France where he remained until 8 February 1918. He was back home again between 9 February and 22 April 1918, before he returned to France for a third time, arriving there the following day. He was eventually demobbed on 21 February 1919.

After the war he lived at 307 High Street, Chatham.

Richard **Croney** was born in 1887. He was a married man, having wed Edith Esther Whitehall on 1 August 1911 at the Registry Office in Chatham. They had three daughters: Edith, who was born on 30 November 1909 out of wedlock, and for whom there was originally a Bastardy Order in place, but which was destroyed on the occasion of Edith's marriage to Richard. Such an order was made out after the birth of the child, outlining who was to pay, how much and for how long. Their second daughter, Elizabeth, was born four months after their wedding on 4 December 1911. The youngest daughter, Emma, was born on 8 August 1915, just four months before Richard enlisted in the Army.

He served with the 1st (Reserve) Garrison Battalion, Suffolk Regiment as Private 31118 and 5746. At the time of his enlistment on 9 December 1915, at Chatham, he was 28 years of age, although he wasn't mobilised until 2 June 1916. On 19 June he was transferred to the 67th (Provost) Battalion, Suffolk Regiment, before being discharged from the Army on 16 September 1916, for no longer being physically fit for war service, having served for 283 days. The reason for this determination was because Richard was suffering with gout, flat feet and a hernia.

After the war he lived at 11 Russell Square Roe Street, Chatham.

Bert George **Giddins** was born in Chatham in 1895. The 1911 Census shows him as a horseman, living with his mother Kate Giddins, his two sisters, Louise and Sarah, and boarders James and Emily Woods, at 39 Rhode Street, Chatham.

There is some confusion surrounding Bert. Army form B.178 which covers an individual's medical history, clearly shows that he underwent a medical examination, which was overseen by the Recruiting Medical Board, at Maidstone on 18 July 1916. The report indicates that he was classified as being unfit due to suffering with kyphosis, *'an abnormal, convex curvature of the spine with a resultant bulge at the upper back.'*

Despite this clear and obvious disability, he was still initially conscripted into the Army on 27 March 1917 at Maidstone, as Private 85799 and 208447, initially joining the 33rd (Works) Battalion, the Middlesex Regiment, which had only been formed in January 1917. This in turn transferred in its entirety to the 6th Battalion, the Labour Corps on 20 April 1917. Despite his initial medical examination, he underwent a second medical at the London General Hospital on 10 August 1917 and a decision was then made that resulted in Bert being discharged from the Army on 26

September 1917 at Nottingham, for no longer being physically fit for war service, having served for 184 days.

Arthur Edward **Goldsmith** was born 1887. Before the outbreak of war, he had been a general labourer. He enlisted at Chatham on 28 November 1914, when he was 27 years of age, serving as Private 4690 with the 3rd Battalion, Queen's Own (Royal West Kent Regiment). Less than a month after enlisting, on Christmas Eve 1914, he was promoted to the rank of lance corporal. On 1 May 1915, he was posted to the regiment's 1st Battalion.

Although the specific details are not known, Arthur had previously served with the Royal Army Medical Corps. He was discharged from the Army on 27 September 1917, for no longer being physically fit for war service, but there was no explanation contained within his medical record as to the specific circumstances which resulted in his being discharged. After the war his address was 4 Hards Town, Chatham.

Sidney George Bruce **Hall** was born in 1875. He married Emma Emily Pynn at Christ Church, Luton, Chatham on 17 October 1897. They had a daughter who was born on 10 August 1900. On 26 August 1916, at Chatham, he began his military service with the Duke of Cambridge's Own 29th Battalion, Middlesex Regiment as Private 38749/53884, at which time he was already 41 years of age. He was not mobilized until 4 September 1916. On 11 October he was transferred to the Depot Company of the Royal Fusiliers and on 21 October he was posted to the regiment's 36th (Labour) Battalion, before being posted back to the Depot Company ten days later.

He served in France as part of the British Expeditionary Force, for only ten days between 21 October and 31 October 1916. He was awarded his Silver War Badge (49571) and certificate on 22 January 1917, and was given a gratuity of £25, a large sum of money at the time, although against that his claim for a weekly Army pension was rejected.

On 22 January 1917, he was discharged from the Army as no longer physically fit for war service, having served for a total of 142 days.

Sydney's wife Emma, wrote a letter to the Infantry Records Office in London, which was received on 23 March 1921. In it she pointed out that she had seen an advertisement in the *News of the World* regarding war time service medals. She requested that any such medals that Sydney was entitled to be sent to them as they had not yet received any. She began the letter by explaining that she was writing on behalf of her *'husband who cannot write on the account of his bad eyesight',* the assumption being that the issue with Sidney's eyes was the reason why he was medically discharged from the Army. It is recorded that on his return from serving in France, he was admitted to Northumberland War Hospital at Gosforth, Newcastle-on-Tyne.

After the war he was living at 2 Alfred Street, Chatham.

Clifford Thomas **Hardy** claimed to have been born in 1896, although it is more than likely he was born in 1901, so he was allegedly 19 when he enlisted in the Army on 20 September 1915 at Canterbury, prior to which he had worked as a printer. Initially he served as Private Hardy (8360 and 3446) with the 3rd Battalion, The Buffs (East Kent Regiment). On 4 February 1916 he was posted to the regiment's 3rd/5th Battalion, and ten days later he was once again posted, this time to A Company, 1st/5th Battalion.

Whilst serving in Bombay, India in June 1916 he contracted jaundice and was admitted to the military hospital in Alexandria on 19 June 1916, before arriving back home in England on 15 July 1916. Clifford was admitted to Holt Auxiliary Hospital in Liverpool on 26 July 1916, suffering with anaemia, malaria and debility. He had contracted the malaria whilst serving with the East Kent Regiment in Mesopotamia. He was a patient at the hospital for thirty days, during which time it was discovered that he had in fact only been 15 years of age at the time of his enlistment and not 19 years and five months as he claimed. Clifford was discharged from the

Army on 20 September 1916 at Canterbury, for *'having made a miss-statement as to age on enlistment',* after having served for a year and a day, which included active service in Mesopotamia.

The following letter was sent by Clifford's mother, Elizabeth Hardy whose husband was Harold Herbert Hardy, a Gunner in the Royal Marine Artillery and a crew member of HMS *Lion*. The letter, which was dated 4 September 1916, read as follows.

'The Commanding Officer 1st/5th Buffs
Re Private Clifford T Hardy No. 3446 'A' Company

Dear Sir,
The above named Private is my son and I wish to claim his discharge from the Army. My reasons are:-
(1). His age is 15 years and 5 months.
(2). He enlisted at the age of 14 without my consent.
(3). He has been abroad and now invalided home.
His proper surname is Perry. The name Hardy is the name of his step-father, who is my husband, now serving on HMS Lion. Should you wish to communicate with him, his full postal address is:-

Gunner H H Hardy
Royal Marine Artillery
HMS Lion
GPO London

PS. Attached please find his birth certificate, which please return.
Elizabeth Hardy'

Harold Herbert Hardy was born on 11 March 1879 and enlisted in the Royal Marine Artillery on 8 July 1897.

The 1911 Census shows Elizabeth Ellen Perry living at 57 Boulton Road, Portsmouth, with her three children, Nellie Emma Jane Perry (11), Clifford Thomas Perry (9) and Harold Leslie Perry (2). Elizabeth had a boarder, who was her future husband, Harold Herbert Hardy.

Some time after having been discharged from the Army, Clifford joined the Mercantile Marine and served during the time of the convoys to Russia.

Although he had previously lived at 14 High Street, Chatham, by 13 January 1919 he had moved to 169 Kingston Road in Portsmouth, where his stepfather, Harold Herbert Hardy, ran a greengrocers. He wrote the following letter to the Infantry Records Office at Hounslow.

'Sir,
I beg to make an application for the Kings Badge. As I have served as a Private on active service with the 1/5 Buffs in Mesopotamia I think that I am entitled to same. As I am serving in the Merchant Service in Russia I think that it will be advisable for it to be sent to my permanent home address.
Believe me.

I am still
Yours obediently
Late Pte. C Hardy
3446 1/5 Buffs'

By 1921 he had moved, and was living at 106 Crasswell Street, Portsmouth. On 14 June 1921, he re-enlisted, this time into the Royal Air Force as Airman 347877.

It is interesting to note that even in official correspondence between the Royal Air Force's Recruiting Depot at White Hart Road Barracks, Portsmouth and the Army's Infantry Record Office, at Hounslow, the only reference as to the actual reason Sidney was discharged from the Army, comes in the form of reference to Paragraph 392 (vi) (a) King's Regulations. In the same letter of correspondence under the heading, 'Medical Category' it still doesn't state the actual reason for his discharge, except to say: *'He was discharged from hospital 24-8-16 (28 days prior to discharge) and was considered fit for Class B, Light Duty, and likely to be fit for service overseas within three months.'*

Although he would need time to recover from the effects of malaria, the above entry seems somewhat strange as it was already known at the time that Clifford had lied about his age on enlistment, so even if his health had improved in three months, the only place he was going was back home to his family and certainly not back to a war zone on foreign soil.

Wallace **Hickmott** was born in Rochester on 15 July 1883. Before the war he had worked in different jobs, including that of an auctioneer, an accountant and a rent and debt collector. On enlistment at Chatham, when he was 33 years of age, he was placed on the Army Reserve and was eventually mobilised on 2 April 1917. He was allocated to the Queen's Own (Royal West Kent Regiment) as Private 26276, but two days later he was transferred to the Army Pay Corps at Chatham in the same rank (12803).

He was admitted to Fort Pitt Military Hospital on 4 September 1917, suffering with chronic psoriasis.

On 22 October 1917 he was discharged from the Army for being no longer physically fit enough for war service, because of his psoriasis condition, having served for a total of one year and 281 days. He had suffered with the ailment for some years. During the short time that he was serving in the Army there was no improvement in his condition and, despite constant treatment, the symptoms had not improved.

William appealed the decision to discharge him due to his long term psoriasis and not award him an Army pension, claiming that his condition had been aggravated by military service. The Pensions Appeal Tribunal heard his case on 12 July 1918 in London, and unanimously decided that his condition was not attributable to, or aggravated by, his military service during the First World War. He was however awarded a one off gratuity payment of £20.

After the war he lived at 33 Military Row, Ordnance Place, Chatham.

John **Holloway** was born in 1876. He had married Florence Beatrice Hurk on 27 August 1888, at All Saints Church, Battle Bridge, Kings

Cross, in Middlesex. Between June 1903 and July 1916, they had six children, the first five of whom were born in Islington, London, with only their youngest child, Charlotte, being born in Chatham.

He enlisted on 12 December 1915 at Chatham, when he was 40 years old and was immediately placed on the Army Reserve. He was eventually mobilized on 13 March 1917 as served as a driver (267811) in the Royal Engineers.

On 30 October 1917, only seven months after being called up, he was discharged from the Army as no longer physically fit enough for war service, with the proviso added under the Military Service (Review of Exceptions) Act 1917, that he was permanently excluded from any liability to be recalled to undertake any future military service.

About four years before he was mobilised, John noticed that he had varicose veins in his right leg. Over time these became more prominent, their condition worsened causing them to swell. He also had to wear a truss for a hernia; it was the combination of the two conditions which ultimately led to his medical discharge. Although both ailments were operable, John refused to have the necessary surgery and, although the Army Medical Board deemed this to be unreasonable, they were not in a position to force him to have an operation.

After the war he lived at 7 Caroline Road, Ordnance Place, Chatham.

Harold George **Kemp** was born at Queensborough, Kent in 1884. He married Florence Maud Harban on 23 May 1915 at the Parish Church in Chatham and was conscripted into the Army on 2 March 1916 at Maidstone, immediately placed on the Army Reserve and then mobilized on 3 July 1918, with the war just four months from its finish. Prior to enlisting he had been a canteen manager. He served with 3rd Company, 5th Battalion, Grenadier Guards as Guardsman 35016.

He was initially placed on the Army Reserve when he was demobilized on 5 February 1919 and then fully discharged on 31 March 1920.

Harold had two periods of hospitalisation, both of which were flu related. He was admitted to the Queen Alexandra Military Hospital, at Millbank in south-west London on 23 October 1918 where he spent a total of fourteen days. He was then transferred to the Devonshire Lodge Auxiliary Red Cross Hospital in Reading to allow him to fully recuperate, as he was still suffering with shortage of breath. So bad was his condition deemed to be by the medical authorities that he spent more than two months as a patient at Devonshire Lodge, although during his time there, he was well enough to be given a twelve-day furlough covering the Christmas period.

After the war he lived at 65 Henry Street, Chatham.

William **Kitchen** was born in 1887 and before the war was a general labourer. He was 27 years old when he enlisted on 10 December 1915 at Chatham. He was immediately placed on the Army Reserve, before being mobilised on 17 January 1916. He became Private 8998 in the 3rd Battalion, The Buffs (East Kent Regiment), but two months later on 21 March 1916, he was discharged from the Army as being unlikely to become an efficient soldier, on medical grounds. He died on 1 May 1917.

In late 1904 William contracted rheumatic fever at Chatham. When he enlisted in the Army he was feeling perfectly well and made no comment about suffering any long term effects of his previous fever. Consequently he was passed as being fit for general service on 10 December 1915. The only slight issue that he noticed was occasionally being short of breath after exercising, but after he had been inoculated, he complained of feeling pain over his heart and suffering from palpitations. It was determined by the medical staff that although William's condition was not as a result of ordinary military service, it was aggravated by it.

After he was discharged from the Army he managed to work for only three weeks before he became confined to his bed and in November 1916 he was admitted to Brompton Hospital. On 21 March 1917 he was awarded a pension of 20s a week for a total of twenty-six weeks.

His home address was 288 High Street, Chatham.

James **Kitchen** was born in 1900. Before the war he worked as a dairyman on a local farm. When he was conscripted into the Army on 20 December 1917 at Maidstone, he was initially placed with No. 365 Reserve Employment Company, but the same day he was re-posted to No. 672 Home Service Employment Company, Labour Corps as Private 461182. Such units usually consisted of soldiers who were either recuperating from wounds or sickness, and not yet fit enough to return to front units, but who were able to carry out work that was classified as 'light duties'.

He was discharged from the Army on 14 March 1918 at Nottingham, having just passed his eighteenth birthday, as no longer fit to undertake war service, after having served for just eighty-five days. It was discovered that he had congenital defective eye sight, which was so bad he had been diagnosed as having 60 per cent disablement.

After the war he was living at 6 Cage Lane, Chatham. Such occurrences do beg the question as to how such a man was passed fit enough for the Army in the first place, when only eighty-five days later he was deemed unfit for war service.

George **Lloyd** was born on 27 September 1884 and before the war had been a transport worker and a sailor in the Mercantile Marine, the forerunner to the Merchant Navy, so it was appropriate for him to serve with the Royal Engineers Transportation Branch, when he was called up on 26 July 1917, as Sapper 318334.

He was medically discharged from the Army on 23 June 1918 in London as no longer physically fit for war service, having served for 333 days. George had hurt his back in a fall when he was in Ramsgate. He fell about 60 feet off the cliff causing severe injuries to his back, after which he had to spend eleven weeks in Broadstairs hospital. Why he was so close to the cliff edge and how it was he came to fall, isn't known. In addition he suffered with chronic bronchitis which, although it had been aggravated by military service, was not the cause of it. He was also suffering with a condition known as hammer toe. Although common, it could be extremely painful, and usually affected the three middle toes leaving them bent in appearance. The condition could be caused by such things as ill-fitting shoes, rheumatoid arthritis and bunions, none of which were good for a soldier.

His claim for an Army pension was heard before an Army Medical Board on 8 April 1919, where he was awarded 5/6 for 52 weeks, which expired on 22 June 1920.

After the war he lived at 15 Priestdale, Chatham.

Frederick George Edmund **Loft** was born in Higham, Kent in 1886. He married Rebekah Boiling on 27 June 1908 at St Nicholas Church in Rochester, with his trade being shown as that of a fishmonger.

Frederick and Rebekah had three sons, Ronald, Frederick and Eric. Their eldest son Ronald, was born on 28 February 1909, Frederick followed eighteen months later, but it would be another six years before Eric was born.

Frederick was conscripted on 24 June 1916 at Chatham when he was 30 years of age, but was not mobilized until 29 November 1916, when he served with the Army Service Corps, Mechanical Transport Section as a private (272296).

He served in France as part of the British Expeditionary Force, arriving at Le Havre on board the SS *King Edward* on 8 January, with the 124th Section Heavy Artillery Motorised Transport. He was also attached to 565th Motorised Transport Section and the 227th Siege Battery, Royal Garrison Artillery for the short time he was in France. He arrived back in England on 19 February 1917 and was at home for only two months before he was medically discharged from the Army on 24 April 1917 at Southport, having served for 305 days.

He had inflammation of the stomach as well as chronic appendicitis, both of which ailments he had before enlistment, yet he was still allowed to join up. It is only possible to make an assumption on how both conditions were missed when Frederick underwent his initial medical, there is also the possibility that both ailments were present at the time but were not as bad then as they later became.

A medical report dated 27 March 1917, which is held on his pension file, states the following: *'Reported sick in France Jan 14, 1917 with pain and vomiting after food, and was admitted to hospital and has been in hospital ever since. He states he has suffered with "stomach trouble" for five years.'*

So serious was Frederick's illness that he had to remain in hospital for ten weeks. Under the heading of *'What is his present condition?'* the following was written.

> *'He complains of pain and vomiting on taking any solid food. There is tenderness on deep pressure over region of appendix. He refuses operation for appendicectomy, he is much debilitated.*
>
> *He will not in my opinion, be fit for any employment in or with the army.'*

The above was written by the officer in charge of the City of London Military Hospital, 42 Clifton Road, Clapton, a major with the Royal Army Medical Corps, and is dated 3 April 1917. The major thought Frederick's refusal to have the required operation was *'most unreasonable'* especially as it meant Frederick would have a permanent disability *'unless he is operated upon.'*

Frederick's decision not to have the operation was a potentially dangerous one, because if his appendix had burst, he would probably die. After the war he was living at 419 High Street, Chatham.

One of Frederick's brothers, Charles, served in the Royal Navy during the war. He was conscripted at Chatham on 22 July 1916, survived the war and was demobbed on 15 September 1919.

Percy **Miller** was born in 1881. He was married on 9 August 1911 at Sleaford, Lincolnshire, to Agatha Munton, with whom he had a daughter, Marjorie, who was born in 1914. Before the war he was a draper's assistant. He was conscripted at the age of 35, on 1 June 1916 at Chatham, but not mobilized until 4 July. He was initially earmarked to join the 3rd Battalion, Royal Sussex Regiment as Private G/13554, but after only eleven days he was transferred to the 1st (Garrison) Battalion, The Buffs (12258), where eventually he acquired the rank of acting corporal. On 30 July 1917 he was transferred again, this time to the 608th Home Service Employment Company, Labour Corps, which was located at Newhaven, as a private (230224). On 23 April 1918, he was once again transferred, this time to the Army Ordnance Corps (41504), but then only six months later he was discharged from the Army for no longer being physically fit enough for war service, due to unexplained fainting attacks. Percy was awarded a pension of 5/6 per week for just twenty-six weeks.

After the war his address was 381 Luton Road, Chatham.

Richard **Page** was born at Chatham in 1880. He was the oldest of four children to Edward and Jane Page, who according to the 1901 Census were living at 85 Hudson Road, Plumstead, London.

He was 37 years old when he began his military service on 9 January 1917 at Eastbourne, and was allocated to serve with the 5th (Reserve) Battalion, Grenadier Guards as Guardsman 27705. He was medically discharged from the Army on 27 August 1917, after serving for only 294 days, as no longer being fit for war service, after the first three fingers of his right hand were amputated in an accident which occurred on 3 June 1917 at Gillingham.

An official medical report on Richard which is dated 3 August 1917, included the following:

> *'When on leave at Gillingham, Kent, he was using a chaff cutting machine; his right hand slipped in among ten knives and the first three fingers were amputated at the second inter phalangeal joints. He was admitted to Fort Pitt Military Hospital on the date of the accident and transferred to Faversham Auxiliary Hospital, a month later, where he remained under treatment until 3 August 1917, when he was sent back to Fort Pitt Hospital.*
>
> *The first and second Phalanges of the first three fingers are amputated, He has full use of thumb and 4th finger but there is limited movement at first three meta-carpo phalangeal joints.'*

Richard was awarded a one-off gratuity payment of £50. After the war he lived at Ashtree Lane, Chatham

David Harold Arthur **Richardson** was born at Chatham in 1897. By trade he was a labourer and he was 19 years old when he was conscripted in March 1916 at Chatham, although he was not called up for service until 17 October 1916, where he became a private (1417) with the Reserve Household Battalion.

He had served in France with the British Expeditionary Force between 3 February and 15 April 1917. On 30 January 1918 he was discharged from the Army for no longer being physically fit for war service, and was also permanently excluded from the requirement to be medically re-examined under the Military Service (Review of Exceptions) Act 1917, after having served for just under two years.

After the war he lived at 28 Middle Street, Chatham, with his parents and his five brothers and sisters.

Charles **Stagg** was born at Gillingham in 1882, and was a 34- year-old labourer when he was conscripted into the Army at Chatham, on 2 June 1916. He wasn't mobilized until 22 July, when he was serving with the Duke of Cambridge's Own Middlesex Regiment as Private 32672.

On 8 December 1906 he married Mercy Catherine Brook at Chatham Registry Office, and over the following eight years, they had four children. During the early years of their marriage, Charles and Mercy lived at 77 Pier Road in Gillingham and Charles was a carriage cleaner on the London, Chatham and Dover Railway.

On 14 October 1916 Charles was discharged from the Army, as it had by then been recognised that he was not likely to become an efficient soldier, on medical grounds, after only having been in the Army for a total of 87 days. The exact reasons for his discharge were not included on his medical report.

After the war Charles, Mercy and their growing family lived at 141 Constitution Road, Chatham.

Arthur Edward **Templeman** was born at Chatham on 27 July 1890. The 1911 Census showed him living at Rose Bungalow, Chestnut Avenue, Walderslade, Chatham, with his parents, Albert and Maria, and his younger brother, John.

He enlisted in the Army on 8 December 1915 and was then immediately placed on the Army Reserve list and wasn't mobilised until 30 January 1917 at Maidstone. Initially he was posted to serve with the 3rd Battalion, The Queen's Own (Royal West Kent Regiment), but was transferred to the Machine Gun Corps on 3 April 1917, and attached to the 148th Company as Private 90420.

After having served his king and country for two years and sixty-six days, which included being part of the BEF in France between 10 August and 4 September 1917, he was discharged from the Army on 11 February 1918 as no longer physically fit for war service due to suffering with epilepsy, for which he required hospital treatment both whilst in France and on his return to England. His journey back home was on board HMHS *St Andrew*, which with its four officers, four nurses and twenty-six staff, usually from the Royal Army Medical Corps, could cater for up to 180 casualties.

Arthur's epilepsy was an ailment which he had had since his childhood, so it can only be assumed that his desire to enlist in the Army was so strong that he didn't inform those who carried out his initial medical about his condition, which was so severe that he was fitting on average every other week. When he returned from serving in France he was admitted to Netley Military Hospital near Southampton, where his epileptic fits were witnessed by the medical staff on more than one occasion.

After the war he lived at 22 Castle Street, Chatham.

Richard Ellington **Williams** was born in Brompton in 1881. He was one of nine children born to Richard and Rebecca Williams.

William was conscripted at Chatham on 2 August 1916, aged 37 years and 8 months, and served with the Royal Engineers as Sapper 185299; four days later he was promoted to the rank of corporal.

On 8 December 1916, he was further promoted to sergeant in the 1st Provost Company, Royal Engineers.

Fortunately both William's service and pension papers have survived, which have provided an in-depth picture of him both as a person and as a soldier. He had previously served with the same regiment, only retiring on 4 April 1916, after a total of 22 years and 72 days when he requested to be discharged, as was his right after having served for such a length of time. His rank at the time was that of corporal (27955). He had originally enlisted for service with the Royal Engineers on 23 January 1894 at Chatham. It was interesting to note that when he initially enlisted as a 15-year-old boy soldier, he was nearly 5ft 2in tall; by the time he re-joined in 1916 as a 37-year-old man, he was shown as being 5ft 10in.

William managed to get himself into the company's conduct book for being a naughty boy on a couple of occasions. An entry for 22 May 1912 read as follows: *'Rendering himself unfit for the performance of his duties by means of indulgence in alcoholic stimulants.'*

Having been found guilty of this breach of discipline, he was severely reprimanded. A repeat of the same behaviour on 16 December the same year saw him placed before a Regimental Court Martial, where he was found guilty, the penalty for which was to be reduced in rank to that of corporal. This time it was whilst he was on board HMT *Rohilla*.

At the time of his enlistment he was living at 21 Bush Street, Chatham and his occupation was that of an electrician. His official enrolment paper had been altered to read Record of Service, and marked 'duplicate'. Under the Military Service Act of 1916, he was deemed to be an ex-soldier who had been recalled for service, rather than somebody who was enlisting in His Majesty's Regular Forces for General Service with the Colours for the first time. For his recall to the Colours, he was awarded a bounty of £25, a substantial sum of money in 1916.

On 26 August 1917, a year and a week after he had been

recalled, he was sent out to Mesopotamia. He had been serving in India as he left Bombay on board the HMT *Kashgar*, on 13 August 1919 and arrived back in the UK on 17 September 1919. He was eventually demobbed from the Army on 30 September 1919, having served with the Royal Engineers for more than twenty-five years.

CHAPTER 7

War Memorials

Most of the war memorials that were erected throughout the United Kingdom after the end of the First World War, were done so in the early 1920s, and for most of the men named on them there was a grave in a cemetery or churchyard somewhere in the world.

The majority of men of the Royal Navy who lost their lives during the war, did so at sea, meaning that for those men, there were no individual graves. For them their final resting place was the inside of a ship or submarine, deep beneath the waves in the waters and oceans around the world. So it was that an appropriate way had to be agreed upon to commemorate such a large loss of life of a nation's young men, who in defence of their county had sacrificed their own futures to safeguard those of others.

A committee was set up by the Admiralty to look at this issue. After much discussion and debate, it was decided that there would be not one, but three identical memorials placed at each of the three 'Manning Ports' that were Plymouth, Portsmouth and Chatham.

Manning Ports were more relevant during the First World War. These were towns that had ports which were home to certain ships and it was also where the men were allocated to a particular ship, but it did not always follow that the Manning Ports only had men who were from that particular town. So all of the sailors who were at Pembroke Barracks at Chatham, didn't all automatically come from the immediate area, they came from all over the country. This

Chatham Naval Memorial (Commonwealth War Graves Commission.

made sense, because that way when a ship was lost at sea, the loss of life that followed did not become a devastating burden on a single community. Such losses had been experienced throughout the country with the raising of Pals battalions, which were eventually scrapped for that very reason. All three of the memorials were designed by Sir Robert Lorimer.

The Chatham Naval Memorial was unveiled on 26 April 1926, by the then Prince of Wales, who later became King Edward VlIl. There are similar memorials at both Plymouth and Portsmouth.

The names of 18,625 British servicemen are commemorated on the memorial, 8,517 of whom were killed during the First World War. The memorial fittingly, overlooks the town of Chatham, its very presence acting as a constant reminder of the price that was paid in blood, pain and death by so many, so that future generations could be free from tyranny.

Besides the Naval Memorial in Chatham there were numerous other war memorials erected across the district, to commemorate the names of all of those local men who fought in the war and paid the ultimate price.

War memorials can be found at the nearby towns of Rochester in the High Street; at Mill Road in Gillingham; at Victoria Gardens in New Road, Chatham; Fort Pitt Cemetery, in City Wall, Chatham; the Dock Road Memorial, in Chatham, as well as the Woodlands Cemetery Memorial in Gillingham.

In the early part of the twentieth century, religion, the local church and God played a major part in everyday life. It was a time when not attending church on a Sunday quite often brought about unfavourable gossip as to the character and type of person an individual was, which in turn reflected negatively on their family. Most churches from the time of the First World War contained Rolls of Honour, recording the names of their parishioners who fell during the war. In some cases these lists can be quite lengthy, showing just how well attended even the smallest of parish churches were.

Gillingham (Woodlands) Cemetery

The Gillingham (Woodlands) Cemetery includes 835 graves from the First World War period, this includes eighty-two men whose identity remains a mystery. The cemetery also includes a war memorial which is inscribed with the names of those local men who lost their lives during the war.

The Royal Naval Hospital, in what was Windmill Hill, was opened on 26 July 1905 by King Edward Vll. A number of those buried in the cemetery had died whilst patients at the hospital. A large section of the cemetery was reserved by the Admiralty for military burials which in the main tended to be men from the Royal Navy, although there were also those who were in the Royal Marines, Royal Marine Light Infantry, Royal Naval Reserve, Royal Air Force and the Royal Marine Labour Corps.

Gillingham (Woodlands) Cemetery (Commonwealth War Graves Commission.

It does not follow that all of those buried in the cemetery are from the Chatham, Gillingham and surrounding areas. Now if a member of the British forces is killed or dies, they are buried in their local churchyard or cemetery, even if their death occurs whilst serving abroad, but during the First World War, men were buried close to where they died. If that was on the battlefields of France or Belgium, then they would have been buried nearby. If they died in a military hospital back home in England, then they would have been buried in a nearby cemetery or churchyard.

Notably the Gillingham Woodlands cemetery is the final resting place for some of the crew of HMS *Bulwark*, which exploded and sank whilst anchored off Sheerness on November 1914, and most of those who were killed in an air raid on the Naval Barracks at Chatham on 3 September 1917. Also buried in the cemetery are those men who served on HMS *Princess Irene* and there is a memorial in the cemetery for these men. The cemetery also has the graves of some of the crew of HMS *Glatton*. The loss of HMS *Bulwark* and the air raid on the Naval Barracks at Chatham are discussed in some detail earlier in this book.

HMS *Princess Irene* was an ocean going liner that had been built for the Canadian Pacific Railway Line in 1914. With the outbreak of the war she was requisitioned by the Royal Navy and converted into a mine-laying vessel. At 1115 hours on 25 May 1915 she was at anchor in the Medway Estuary, halfway between Sheerness and Chatham, undergoing refitting in preparation of an operation that she was about to embark on. Without any warning and with catastrophic consequences, HMS *Princess Irene* exploded, with flames and heavy smoke reaching hundreds of feet into the air. When the columns of smoke had cleared, there was not a vestige of the vessel still visible, she had simply disappeared. A total of 273 of the crew were killed, along with 76 dockyard workers, including shipwrights, apprentices and boys. Three other civilians who were working inland at the time were also killed. Wreckage from the vessel was found as far as 20 miles away.

HMS Princess Irene.

Government tug boats and other vessels were rushed down from Chatham and Sheerness in the hope of helping with survivors, but to no avail. Instead all they could do was to search for the bodies of those who had been killed. Only a small number of bodies of those killed were ever found, with most of the men coming from either Sheerness or Chatham. Three badly mutilated bodies were discovered, one of them was headless. One of the bodies was subsequently identified as that of a Mr Turner of Chatham, by means of a letter that was found in his jacket pocket. Henry Turner was 47 years old and a skilled dockyard labourer. He and his wife Jessie, who had married in the town on 29 April 1893, lived at 102 Luton Road, Chatham, with their four children, Harry, Jessie, May and Eva.

The force of the explosion was such that the ceiling of a house at Eastchurch, which is 10 miles away from the where the explosion was, collapsed.

The dockyard workers who lost their lives were:

Shipwrights

J. Riton, W. Falk, A. Wiseman, R. Burrows, H. Grout, J. Stride, F. Lott, J. Rogers, P. Young, N. Barling, H. Smith, F. Branchett, R. Stirling, F. Clachett, U. Keeble, R. Wood, L. Turner, J. Stephens, G. Slade, F. Brazil, W. Chittock, F. Adams, H. Farley, J. Daniels, P. Harness, R. Trowell, R. Jenner, J. Rowswell, J. Wigley, T. Proom, W. Gamblin, H. Stevens, E. Hawkins, R. Irons.

Apprentices

A. Newman, J. Grant, C. Daws, S. Bridge, J. Goulding, S. Poyke, R. Howell.

Skilled Labourers

F. Noades, W. Susans, J. Blae, H. Nokes, C. Clay, M. Wood, F. Brown, J. Mills, J. Deal, H. Black, A. Akhurst, D. Clancy, J. Collins, J. Bourne, H. Brown, A. Barton, J. O'Callaghan, W. Smith, F. Kember, H. Lawrence, A. Burgess, W. Keem, J. Buckhurst, E. Callaghan, W. Bidford, G. Watts, H. Turner.

Boys

B. Snelling, J. Brown, W. Harrison.

Only one member of the crew, who was on board the vessel at the time of the explosion, is known to have survived, that was Stoker David Wills, who was rescued by the tug boat *Bruno*. Three other crew members, William James Paice, John P. Sutton and James Thompson, survived, but only because they were not on board the vessel at the time of the explosion.

The explosion also resulted in the death of 9-year-old Hilda Johnson, who was on holiday in the Isle of Grain at a relative's house. At the time of the explosion she was playing in the garden when a piece of metal from the exploding ship struck her on the head.

Close by, the body of a local workman, 47-year-old George Bradley, was discovered in a potato field. His death was attributed to the sudden shock of hearing the ship explode.

A local electrical fitter, Mr Potter, also died in Sheerness Hospital where he had gone to have his wounds treated after having been struck by debris falling from the sky.

A court of inquiry decided that a faulty primer was to blame for the explosion, not helped by the priming of the mines being undertaken, supposedly by untrained personnel. In times of war suspicion in such matters always leans towards the possibility of sabotage, especially when similar incidents had befallen other vessels. In this case a worker at Chatham Dockyard was actually named as a suspect in all of the explosions, but after a thorough investigation by Special Branch, the man was released and cleared of any such involvement.

Brompton War Memorial

The Brompton War Memorial is located near to the Royal School of Military Engineering, which can be found on the village green immediately next to Brompton Barracks in Gillingham. The memorial was unveiled by Major General H.F. Fuller on 1 March 1921.

The names listed below are those which are recorded on the war memorial and do not include the names of local men who were casualties of the war, who for whatever reason were never included on it. Sadly this is an all too common occurrence, where for different reasons, names have been inadvertently omitted from their local war memorial.

F.C. Baldwin
Percy Frank Baldwin
William Joseph Barnes
William A. Bass
William Arthur Bennett
Charles Henry Berry
T. Butler
William Job Clarke
Frederick T. Climo
John James Cook
Patrick Coyne
William Frances Crust
Ernest Charles Dawson
A.W. Doyle
A.H. Goodchild
Joseph Patrick Hamill
William Patrick Hamill
William James Harbour
Frederick William Hughes
Robert Patrick Kinnear
Frederick John Matthems
John Anthony McCudden MC
James Thomas B. McCudden VC, DSO & Bar, MC & Bar, MM
William Thomas James McCudden
J.H. Neal
E.J. Neal
William Joseph Price
Joseph Redgrave

Cecil John Robbins
C. Robins
Victor Rogers
Edward Russell
Frederick William Edward Sandford
R. Scott
William Henry Shrubb
David Colin Simpson
Oliver George Stace
W.H. Stace
John Charles Sullivan
George E. Spicer
Herbert Douglas Summers
Charley George Sutton
John William Tebble
Victor Stephen Tebbles
George Patrick Tomlin
J. Tomlin
J.H. Wheeler
Thomas Robert Williams
W.J.C. Williams
Archibald Wilmot

The Gillingham War Memorial was originally erected and unveiled on 20 July 1924, somewhat uniquely it must be said, in the middle of a roundabout at the top of Mill Road. Vehicular traffic at the time was of course only a fraction of what it is today. It was eventually moved to the nearby Medway Park.

The memorial was unveiled by Alderman W.H. Griffin, JP and the dedication, to the memory of the names of the men it represented, was conducted by the Bishop of Rochester, J. Harmer. Those present included local dignitaries, retired servicemen, the friends and relatives of men who had died and been killed during the First World War, as well as ordinary members of the local community, as can be seen from the photograph on the next page.

Sadly the memorial does not include the individual names of the very men it was put in place to commemorate.

Gillingham War Memorial.

Gillingham War Memorial.

Victoria Gardens War Memorial, Chatham

The War Memorial in the town's Victoria Gardens, comes in the shape of a Celtic cross and is the location where the town's Remembrance Day parade and service takes place each year. The memorial commemorates all of those men who gave their lives in

Victoria Gardens War Memorial.

defence of their country during both World Wars, but does not include their individual names. It carries the simple yet poignant inscription *'Lest we Forget'*.

Victoria Gardens first opened as a public park in 1897 and was part of Queen Victoria's Diamond Jubilee celebrations. It had previously been owned by the British War Department which sold it to the Corporation of Chatham in the early 1890s when landscaping and tree planting was carried out. It had a bandstand for musical concerts throughout the summer months, which were always very popular with members of the general public.

Postscript

When the Armistice came at 11am on 11 November 1918 there was rejoicing that the war was finally over after four and a half long bloody years. During that time hundreds of men who were connected with Chatham, either because they lived there, were born there or were stationed there, had been killed and hundreds more had been wounded. Wives had been widowed and children had been orphaned to ensure victory over the Germans in an effort to secure a peace for future generations to enjoy, but the reality was that the hard won peace would be sustained for only twenty years before it would happen all over again; the Second World War was born out of the ashes of the first.

Whatever the cost and no matter how painful it had been for everybody concerned, life had to go on and return to some kind of normality, although for many there could be no going back to what had been their normality. People wanted and expected more out of life, especially after the dreadful price they had paid during the course of the war.

Five young Buglers

Even though the war was over, many young men were still in uniform, most of whom were simply waiting to be demobbed. Stopping them from becoming bored and ill-disciplined wasn't an easy task.

An article appeared in the national newspapers, on 17 January 1919, about five young buglers from the Royal West Kent Regiment who had broken into the Waggon at Hale public house in Capstone

Road, Chatham, stole a cash box containing £40 in notes and change and made good their escape. Why the five young men carried out the crime isn't clear, but they certainly weren't looking to become rich, as they supposedly shared their ill-gotten gains with twenty-one other buglers back at their camp.

After the five were arrested, the Police managed to recover £20 of the monies that had been stolen. Other than the fact that all five of the men were sent for trial, the outcome of the case wasn't included in the article or how it was that those responsible for the crime were originally identified.

General Election 1918

A month after the end of the First World War, Great Britain saw its first post war general election, which took place on Saturday, 14 December 1918, becoming the first such vote to take place over just one day. Because of the number of men who were still serving in the armed forces overseas, the full count did not take place until 28 December.

The previous Member of Parliament for Chatham, who had been elected in January 1910, was the Conservative Party politician, Gerald Fitzroy Hohler, who had defeated the town's first Labour MP, John Jenkins, and had served throughout the war years. In the 1918 election he sat for and won the newly formed seat at Gillingham as a Coalition Conservative candidate, rather than run again for the Chatham seat. He held the Gillingham seat for the next three Parliaments, before finally standing down at the 1929 election. He was knighted in 1924.

John Moore-Brabazon.

The newly elected MP for Chatham in 1918, and the man whom the electorate of the town had decided was the best person to take them into the uncertainty of the post war years, was John Moore-Brabazon, 1st Baron Brabazon of Tara. He won the seat with a majority of 7,320 votes, nearly treble the number of votes won by the Labour candidate who was the runner up. He was an interesting character to say the least.

John Moore-Brabazon, with his Voisin Bird of Passage in Leysdown, Kent in 1909.

He was born John Theodore Cuthbert Moore-Brabazon, on 8 February 1884 in London. His parents, Lieutenant Colonel John Arthur Henry and Emma Sophia Moore-Brabazon, were wealthy enough to have him educated at Harrow School followed by Cambridge University, where he studied engineering.

From an early age John Moore-Brabazon had always been fascinated by speed and in 1907 he won the Circuit des Ardennes car race at Bastogne in Luxembourg, driving a Minerva, which was a Belgian luxury vehicle. He was 23 years of age. Not content with the experience of speed on a racetrack, he wanted even more of a challenge, so in 1908 he took himself off to France where he learnt to fly in a Voisin biplane, named after its manufacturer and aeronautical engineer, Gabriel Voisin. On 2 May 1909 he became the first Englishman to make an officially recognised flight at Shellbeach on the Isle of Sheppey, when he flew a distance of 1,500 feet.

Nearly six months later on 30 October, he won a prize of £1,000, which had been offered by the *Daily Mail* to the first person who could fly the distance of a mile. He also holds the distinction of being the first person to qualify as a pilot in the UK, which he achieved on 8 March 1910, his flying certificate being allocated the number one, to commemorate this achievement.

With the outbreak of the First World War he joined the Royal Flying Corps as a second lieutenant and by the end of the war, and by now serving in the newly formed Royal Air Force, he had reached the rank of temporary lieutenant colonel, which was made substantive on 1 January 1919. He served on the Western Front, carrying out both reconnaissance and aerial photography, for which he was twice mentioned in despatches on 15 October 1915 and 13 November 1916. In February 1916, he was awarded the French military decoration the *Legion d'Honneur*. On New Year's Day 1917, he was awarded the Military Cross for an act of bravery.

He remained the MP for Chatham until 1929, serving the town with both pride and due diligence.

Wife's tragic discovery

An article in the local newspapers in March 1919 carried the sad story of Captain Cowley of the Royal Engineers, who lived in Marlborough Road, Gillingham and who was found dead by his wife, in the scullery of his home. The article said;

> *'It is supposed that returning home without his latch key, he entered the house by the scullery window. The gas tap in the scullery was turned on, but it is not clear whether that caused his death.'*

Further research showed that Captain Cowley, was 41-year-old Francis Llewellyn Cowley, and that he worked at the Royal School of Military Engineering, in Pasley Road, Gillingham. His wife's name was Lily, and after the war she was living at 'Floriana', 136 Gillingham Road, Gillingham. He had apparently died of heart failure on 18 March 1919.

Chatham Suicides

June 1919 was a sad time for at least two Chatham families: the Coulthorps and the Huthwaites. In each case a son from each family committed suicide, but what connected the two cases was that on both occasions the man concerned was the third brother from each of the families to have committed suicide. In an even sadder twist the three Huthwaite brothers had all committed suicide by slitting their own throats, whilst the three Coulthorp brothers had all taken their own lives by gassing themselves in the same oven.

Tar and Feathers

When this matter was first reported in the press, there wasn't much detailed information, which made the story seem a strange affair, but by the middle of June 1919, the picture had become much clearer. The story had started out with two Naval officers and another man, who was the brother of one of the men, and resulted in one of the officers being tarred and feathered by his fellow officer and his brother.

All that had been reported initially was that one of the officers – Sub-Lieutenant Desmond B. Kinahan – had been tarred and feathered by Lieutenant Francis Thomas Wright and his brother, but no reason was given as to why this had taken place. The article went on to explain that Kinahan was looking to make a criminal complaint of assault against his colleague, despite the fact that his own senior officers were strongly advising him not to make any contact with the press over the matter.

It was intriguing to read about as it was blatantly clear that there was a strong reason behind why the tarring and feathering had actually taken place. It became even more intriguing when Lieutenant Wright, the person accused by Kinahan of assaulting him, admitted he was guilty of the allegation against him and was seeking the maximum publicity possible. An article in the press dated 18 June 1919, cleared up the matter:

> **Husband Placed Under Open Arrest**
> *'A new development took place on Tuesday in connection with the tarring and feathering of the naval officer, Sub-Leut. Kinahan, during Friday night. Lieut. Francis Wright, whose wife's name has been mentioned with that of the naval officer, has been placed under open arrest by the local APM, who has acted on instructions from headquarters. Lieut. Kinahan has been sent by the naval authorities to Chatham Naval Barracks.*
>
> *Lieut. Wright is still living at his home in Cambridge, but he has to report himself every morning. He is anything but concerned over the arrest. He declares that he is seeking the fullest publicity, and adds that if he is not sent to a court-martial by the authorities he will himself ask to be sent. On the other hand the naval authorities who are, so to speak, the guests of the University, are very anxious to hush the matter up.*
>
> *There are still many rumours about the affair, but Lieut. Wright himself says: "I deliberately tarred and feathered Desmond Kinahan because he stole my wife while I was away."*
>
> *Sub-Lieut. Desmond Kinahan stated on Friday night at the Naval Barracks, Chatham, that he intended to bring an action for assault against Lieut. Wright in connection with the tarring and feathering affair.'*

Lieutenant Wright had served in Salonika during the war where he was awarded the Military Cross for his bravery. His brother, who helped him carry out the feathering and tarring, had also served during the war, and lost a leg and was badly wounded in one arm. They carried out the attack on Sub-Lieutenant Desmond Kinahan, aged 20, because of his close friendship with Lieutenant Wright's wife.

Kinahan was described as being an immaculate dresser who enjoyed dancing immensely, particularly jazz, a pleasure which took him to some of London's best known musical clubs and bars. He had a wide circle of friends in his home town of Cambridge, and was by all accounts an attractive young man who did not find it difficult to attract members of the opposite sex. His father was at the time a serving officer in His Majesty's armed forces.

In April 1919, Lieutenant Wright's brother gave an interview to the press about the matter:

> *'Two months ago I went and told the naval officer what I thought about him, and he promised he would not see my sister-in-law until he had seen my brother. He gave me a written statement. As far as we knew, he had kept his promise. About six weeks after my brother came home from Salonika, and we went and interviewed the Lieutenant in his rooms.*
>
> *At my brother's request he gave up some letters written to him, photographs, and presents. Afterwards we were told of a further meeting.*
>
> *On Thursday my brother and I went up to London and bought a chain 15 feet long and weighing 25lb, and we also purchased the stoutest padlock we could get. We also obtained a gallon of tar from the local gas works and a bag of feathers from a farm.*
>
> *We wrote to Lieutenant Kinahan and asked him to meet us at 10.30pm on Friday at our house. When he came we asked him to go in to the garage.*
>
> *He was asked if he would take it quietly. My younger brother was present in case he was needed. Lieutenant Kinahan, however took off his jacket and waistcoat himself, and my brother pulled off his shoes, socks and trousers. He was sitting on the ground and he took off his own tie and collar, we folded up his clothing, placing in his pockets his personal property, and taking the greatest care not to lose or damage anything.*
>
> *I would also like to say that though we tarred him completely we were very careful not to injure him in any way, and kept the stuff from his nose, eyes and ears. It is not quite accurate to say that he was nude, because he was well covered with feathers. We then put a heavy chain round his neck and asked him to step in to the car. This he did without resistance.*

> *The story of how he was found has already been related. The leaflets distributed from the car were prepared the day before.*
>
> *Had Kinahan been a big man, my brother would have thrashed him first and shot him afterwards. That was his intention when he came home, but he was such a rabbit that we decided to do the other thing.'*

Lieutenant Wright had married in October 1918 after having known his wife for less than six weeks. They had only been married for a matter of weeks before his leave was over and he had to return to his unit abroad. When he found out about her having been seen out with Kinahan, he wrote to her, offered to forgive her and take her back. Her reply of 'Never, never, never', was possibly not the answer he was expecting to hear.

Kinahan was found tarred, feathered and chained to a tree in Cambridge. Remarkably the Police did not take any action in the matter, but instead were more than happy for the Navy to deal with the matter internally.

Desmond B. Kinahan had previously served on board HMS *Britannia*, the vessel which had been sunk on 9 November 1918, off Cape Trafalgar, Spain, two days before the Armistice was signed. She was sunk by a torpedo which had been fired by the German U-boat, *UB-50*. A total 712 officers and men survived the sinking, but another 50 were killed and a further 80 were injured.

The ship's commander was Captain Francis F. Caulfield RN. After the *Britannia* started listing, a fire broke out below decks, which caused the cordite in one of the magazines to explode. It was two and a half hours before she finally sank and this allowed time for many officers and men to escape.

Chatham's least favourite son and the Cornish Murders

This story relates to a man who was born in Chatham, lived in the town until he was about 10 years old and then moved away never to return. The reason it is included is because of what he did after

HMS Britannia.

he returned home from the war having been held as a prisoner of war by the Turks.

The man in question was Henry Perry, who also used the surname of his stepfather, Beckett – his crime, murder, not just once, but four times. What made the murders even more heinous, was the bloody and barbaric way in which he took the lives of his four victims and the fact that they were, by marriage, all related to him. Chatham Perry is one of the worst English murderers of the First World War years.

A point worth noting is the speed with which this case took place, starting with the murders on 28 April 1919, to Perry's interview and confession on 3 May 1919 and his subsequent execution on 10 July

1919, just ten weeks and three days later. A comparison case today would more than likely take around eighteen months before it reached the trial stage at Crown Court.

How Perry was identified as a suspect and where and how he was subsequently discovered is not clear, but he was interviewed at East Ham Police station by Detective Chief Inspector Neil and Detective Inspector Hall, after which he made a statement. Here are some extracts from it:

> *'As far as I remember I was born at Chatham. My father was a sailor, and he died when I was young. My mother married a hawker named Beckett. While I was still very young we used to travel the country in a caravan. On November 29th 1916, I joined the 3rd Suffolks at Bury St Edmunds, and done my training and Felixstowe, and was drafted early in 1917 to Egypt. I was stationed at Stidi Bish, near Alexandria, and in about six weeks we were then sent to Palestine on the Gesrea–Beersheba front. Some time in May 1917 I went out to get some water, when I got lost. I rambled about all night, and next morning I was overtaken by some Arabs, and while walking along I was fired at by a Turkish Bedouin. I was slightly wounded in the left leg. I was taken prisoner and taken to a Turkish camp.'*

The statement continued with Perry explaining the remaining period of his time as a prisoner and his long journey home, finally arriving at Southampton on 26 February 1919. At different times he claimed to be part of the Australian Expeditionary Force and a returning prisoner of war. He then travelled up to Ipswich to see his sister, Mrs Louie Smith, before arriving in London to stay with his step-aunt, Mrs Mary Cornish at 13 Stukeley Road in Forest Gate. Here he murdered the entire family: Walter Cornish, 47, and his wife Alice, 43, and their children, Alice, 14 and Marie, 5.

Perry then starts to explain how he carried out the four murders on 28 April 1919:

> *'I was passing Mrs Cornish's door. She called me in and gave me one or two rough words, and asked me to stop to dinner. I*

lost my temper and knocked her down with the kitchen poker. I carried her into the shed at the bottom of the garden. She was not dead but unconscious. I hit her with a pickaxe and went back in to the house, got a carving fork from the drawer, and stabbed her in the throat. This would be between 2 and 3 pm. I covered her over with some boards and rubbish and then went back to the house and remained there until the little girl Marie came in from school. I hit her on the head with a hammer in the passage. She fell down, and I struck her again, then picked her up and threw her down the cellar. Soon after Alice came in from school. I let her in. She went into the kitchen. I struck her on the head with the hammer, She fell down, and then I hit her on the throat with an axe and carried her into the cellar.

I waited until Mr Cornish came in from work. He said to me, "What games are you having, I am going to hand you over to the Police." We had a few words because he was annoyed at me being there. He turned his back, and I hit him on the head with the axe as I hit the girl Alice with. I struck him a second time, but he got away and was frightened and went out of the house.'

The statement continued with a clear description of how he spent the monies that he had stolen from the house after committing the murders. As a document it is graphic in both its clarity and content and portrays Perry as a somewhat calm and thoughtful individual. In 1919 a suspect's statement wasn't written down verbatim or tape recorded by the officer concerned. Instead he would listen to what he was being told by the suspect, make hand written notes and the write them up as best he could recall. The suspect would then sign to confirm that the words contained in the statement were a true reflection of what he had actually said.

The brutality of each murder is almost made worst by Perry's apparent calmness and indifference to what he has just done, whilst waiting for his next victim to arrive home.

Whether Perry's actions were affected in any way by what is today referred to as Post Traumatic Stress Disorder is not known, although during the First World War, it was known as shell shock, war neurosis or combat stress. All that can be said is that it is possible his behaviour in carrying out these horrific murders was affected by his war time experiences, in what he had witnessed and how he had been treated whilst a prisoner of war of the Turkish.

Before enlisting in the Army he had seventeen criminal convictions for different crimes including violence. The 1911 Census records that at the time he was incarcerated in His Majesty's Prison Princetown.

At his subsequent trial at the Old Bailey in the City of London, on 27 May 1919, in front of His Honour Mr Justice Darling, Perry's barrister put forward a plea of insanity as a way of explaining his behaviour, claiming that he was beaten and tortured whilst he was held as a prisoner of war by the Turkish, although there was absolutely no mention of this in Perry's original statement to the Police, soon after his arrest. The jury found him guilty of all four murders.

Clive Emsley's book, entitled *Violent crime in England in 1919*, quoted the trial prosecutor in the Perry case, Percival Clarke, as having said:

> *'The war has done great good for some persons, it has taught them discipline, and made honest and honourable men of people who started badly. But the brutalities of war may have made more vicious a person who was vicious before'.*

Perry's execution was carried out by John Ellis, who first served as an assistant executioner in 1901 and went on to serve as the Chief Executioner from 1907 until 1924. Having been involved in a total of 203 executions, Ellis committed suicide in September 1932 by cutting his throat with a razor.

Chatham's future

One of the issues to hit Chatham after the war was a cut in jobs, many of which were lost in the naval dockyards, which no longer required the large number of war time workers that had been employed there. To a large extent it was simple economics, which had always been a likely consequence once the war had ended, even if nobody wanted to admit it. It was an unwanted by-product of winning the war.

On 9 July 1919 a meeting took place at Chatham Dockyard, when representatives from the Corporations at Chatham, Rochester and Gillingham met with the Lords of the Admiralty, in an effort to try and establish what the future of Chatham Dockyards was and how that would affect the jobs of men who relied on it for their livelihood. The Mayor of Chatham also attended the meeting.

With the obvious forthcoming large scale reduction in work connected to a loss of jobs in the building and repairing of warships, the representatives from the three towns were requesting that a local industry be established, so as to replace the jobs that had been lost. The First Lord of the Admiralty could provide no such reassurances, but he did promise the deputation of local representatives that Chatham would receive a fair share of future national work. What that actually meant in reality, wasn't made clear.

What eventually happened in relation to the long term jobs issue in the dockyard also had a knock on effect in respect of housing in Chatham. During the war the dockyard was full of workmen, with the result that housing accommodation in and around the Chatham area, had been heavily taxed, but once the war ended the building of new housing slowed down considerably.

At the end of the war building schemes for housing were in hand for certain areas on the outskirts of Chatham, but the local authorities were reluctant to allow them to proceed any further, until they had also received assurances from the Admiralty that the dockyard would not be badly affected by the end of the war.

Fatal fall after Peace Celebrations

A verdict of 'accidental death' was the outcome of the inquest which took place at the Chatham Royal Naval Hospital, into the tragic death of 19-year-old Ordinary Seaman, Hector Reuben Taylor, who died on the evening of Saturday, 19 July 1919, at the end of the town's peace celebrations.

Ordinary Seaman Taylor was a member of the crew of HMS *Dragon*, which was moored in Chatham Harbour. Along with some of his colleagues he was assisting to undress the ship, but instead of descending the mast by a Jacob's rope ladder, he slid down an iron stay and crashed on to the deck, fatally injuring himself in the process.

He is buried at the Kingston-upon-Thames Cemetery, in Surrey.

30-Knot Super Cruiser

Thursday, 24 July 1919 saw the commissioning of the new British cruiser *Hawkins*, which was the first of her class to be completed. She was destined for service as one of the flagships at the China station. The Hawkins design was universally accepted as being a great advance on all other types of light cruiser of that time. Her design was so advanced that she was the same size as an armoured cruiser from the very early years of the twentieth century. Although more heavily armoured, she had a much faster speed.

The Kent cruiser of 1906 had a top speed of 21,000 hp, which meant that she had a maximum speed of 21 knots. The more powerful engines of the new Hawkins class cruiser provided a top speed of 30-knots, making her an all-round faster and much more dynamic vessel.

In closing

I hope that you have enjoyed this relatively brief account of what Chatham was like during the years of the First World War, and the men from the town who fought and died in it. In a book such as this it is not possible to cover every aspect of the war and the effect that it had on Chatham. Hopefully what you have read has proved both useful and informative and whetted your appetite to find out more.

Index

Aboukir, HMS, 20–1, 61
Adams, William John, 94
Allen, Arthur, 48
Allery, Private Henry Thomas, 88
Arnold, Alfred, 95
Amphion, HMS, 16–17
Andrews, Henry Richard, 48
Arethusa, HMS, 19, 45–7

Balfour, Arthur, 80
Barnard, William, 96
Barrage Balloon Station, 88
Beaumont, Sidney Robert, 96
Beckett, Robert, 97
Bending, Cecil James, 51
Bending, Sydney John, 51
Biggs, Thomas Ronald, 82
Blogg, Archdeacon Oswald William Charles, 41
Bluejackets, 80
Boscawen, Colonel Sir Arthur, 39
Brady, John, 97
Branch, Corporal William Joseph, 87
Britannia, HMS, 141
Brompton Barracks, 30
Brompton War Memorial, 127
Brown, Frank, 98
Buckley, William Thomas, 81
Bulwark, HMS, 22–4
Butcher, Charles Battlemore, 48

Castle, Albert, 99
Chatham Naval Memorial, 122
Chapell, Henry John, 99
Cheeseman, Harry, 100
Cherry, Harry, 101
Cockburn, Sir John, 44
Cooper, Miss Catherine, 54–5, 57
Coster, William George, 102
Cramp, James, 102
Credland, Harold, 79
Cressy, HMS, 20–2, 61
Crisp VC DSO, Thomas, 60
Croney, Richard, 103
Cummings, James, 48, 49

Dibley, Private Charles, 34
Dogger Bank, Battle of, 27, 47, 52
Doon, HMS, 79
Drummond, Captain John, 21
Duncan, HMS, 30

Earle, Austin Mostyn, 17

Ford Park Cemetery, Plymouth, 30
Formidable, HMS, 27–8
Fort Amhurst, 12
Fort Pitt, Military Hospital, 11–13, 77
Franks, Lieutenant, 77
Fraser, James, 79
Fraser, Lieutenant Commander Harry Macleod, 79–80
French, Lord, 67

Gardiner, Mr Gideon, 66
George V, King, 78
George, Prime Minister David Lloyd, 61
George, William, 40
Giddins, Bert George, 104
Gillingham War Memorial, 130
Gillingham (Woodlands) Cemetery, 123
Goldsmith, Arthur Edward, 105

Haldane, Lord Chancellor, Viscount, 79
Hall, Sidney George Bruce, 105
Hammond, Reverend L.D., 32
Handford, Douglas Frederick, 83
Hardy, Clifford Thomas, 106
Hardy, Harold Herbert, 107
Harling, William, 48
Harrad, George, 83
Harris, George, 56
Harris, Lord George, 37
Harvey VC, Major Francis John William, 51–2
Hickmott, Wallace, 109
Hicks, Gunner Charles, 56
Hogue, HMS, 20, 61
Holloway, John, 109
Horton War Hospital, 19

James, Trevor, 84
Jeffery, Arthur Henry, 84
Jeffery, William Thomas, 84

Keilback, Lieutenant Hans, 35
Kemp, Harold George, 110
Kitchen, James, 112
Kitchen, William, 111
Kunigin Luise, SMS, 17

Langton, Reverend H.R., 18
Lewis, Lieutenant Cyril William Victim, 73, 75
Liberty, HMS, 20
Lion, HMS, 52
Lloyd, George, 112

Loft, Frederick George Edmund, 113
Longley, George Charles, 68–9
Loxley, Captain Noel, 29
Lutzow, SMS, 52

Marlborough, Duke of, 12
McSweeney, James, 18
Mile End Military Hospital, 19
Miller, Percy, 114
Moore-Brabazon, John, 134–5
Murdoch, Lance Corporal J., 37
Murray, Sir Oswyn, 68

Neuve-Chapelle, Battle of, 27
Nicholls, Ernest Walter, 48
Nicholson, Captain Wilmot, 21

Osborn, George, 85

Page, Richard, 115
Paine, Alderman W., 37
Pembroke, HMS, 62, 69
Perry, Henry, murderer, 140–4
Poore, Lieutenant Roger, 38
Prince of Wales, HMS, 24
Princess Irene, HMS, 125
Pritchard, Private Nathaniel, 87

Reed, Frederick William, 85
Richards, Captain Walter Hayes Pickering, 32
Richards, William John, 86
Richardson, David Harold Arthur, 116
Robinson, Richardson, 48
Royal Garrison Artillery, 15
Royal Naval Volunteer Reserve, 16

Saunders, Sapper Thomas Henry, 33
Sharp, Harry, 72
Sharp, Horace Stanley, 72
Sleeth, Leonard, 48
Smith, Private David, 86
Smith, Private Walter Henry, 14
Stagg, Charles, 116
Stowell, William Thomas, 18

Tanner, Private Ernest, 87
Taylor, James Thomas Andrew, 48
Templeman, Arthur Edward, 117
Thelen, Lieutenant Otto, 35
Trest, HMS, 79
Trigg, Emily Maria, 53, 57
Turley, Stoker 2nd Class Wilfred Alfred, 31
Turner, Ethelbert Palmer, 48
Turner, Private Henry Francis Charles, 88
Turpin, Frederick W., 66

Turner, Sydney, 58

UB-122, 81

Vanguard, HMS, 61
Victoria Gardens War Memorial, 131
Villers-Bretonneux Memorial, 84

Warley Barracks, 19
Warne, William George, 48
Waveney, HMS, 79
Wightman, Henry, 48
Wilkinson, Tom, 77
Williams, Richard Ellington, 117
Winston Churchill, 19
Woodlands Cemetery, Gillingham, 70
Woolnough, Private Charles, 86
Woolnough, Sergeant Thomas Henry, 86